THE MODERN
CORPORATION
AND SOCIAL
RESPONSIBILITY

*Third in the sixth series of Rational Debates
sponsored by the American Enterprise Institute
held at
American Enterprise Institute
Washington, D. C.*

ROBERT GORALSKI
Moderator

THE MODERN CORPORATION AND SOCIAL RESPONSIBILITY

Henry G. Manne
Henry C. Wallich

RATIONAL DEBATE SERIES

American Enterprise Institute for Public Policy Research
Washington, D. C.

Library of Congress Catalog Card Number L.C. 72-91865

THE MODERN CORPORATION
AND SOCIAL RESPONSIBILITY

Henry G. Manne
and
Henry C. Wallich

Published by
American Enterprise Institute for Public Policy Research

The idea that business enterprises have broader responsibilities than the production and sale of goods and services has been a fixture of American social-reformist thinking for some time. This idea is generally labeled "corporate social responsibility," and today, as concern over our deteriorating natural and social environments spreads, the phrase becomes more common in public discourse.

But just what is meant by corporate social responsibility? What are its implications for public policy? In this, the twenty-third in a continuing series of Rational Debates presented by the American Enterprise Institute, Professors Henry G. Manne and Henry C. Wallich grapple with this important and difficult concept.

Professor Manne, Kenan professor of law at the University of Rochester, says that since its modern introduction in the early thirties, the concept "has enjoyed periodic and substantial vogue in the business world" as a means "to counteract public hostility towards business," the focus of business "altruism" shifting with the "social and economic concerns of the broader public."

The cornucopia of the corporate social responsibility advocates overflows with a vast array of programs and proposals but, according to Dr. Manne, this is not where the "real economic or social significance" of the concept is to be found. A list of such proposals reveals nothing about the "economic implications of this doctrine." Is corporate altruism feasible; are corporate decision makers likely to make "unselfish" decisions; and can voluntary corporate action "really accomplish its announced goals?"

Answering these questions requires a working definition of corporate social responsibility. Dr. Manne offers one with three elements: To qualify as socially responsible corporate action, a business expenditure or activity must be "one for which the marginal returns to the corporation are less than the returns available from some alternative expenditure," must be purely voluntary, and must be an actual corporate expenditure rather than a conduit for individual largess.

Even with such a definition in mind, says Professor Manne, "in practice it is often extremely difficult if not impossible to distinguish a purely business expenditure only alleged to have been made for the public's good from one actually made with real charitable intent."

What of the proponents of business social action? In Dr. Manne's view they come from three main groups. There are the government officials who are always willing to "claim credit for all public benefits and accept no responsibility for increased costs and long-run antisocial effects." There are the "intellectuals of the left" for whom the idea has become a "convenient peg on which to hang every hackneyed criticism of business conduct and even a few new ones." But the "most important group . . . [is comprised of] businessmen themselves, particularly executives of larger corporations." For this last group—although there are secondary motivations—"corporate social responsibility is good business because it is good public relations."

Dr. Manne doubts the feasibility and effectiveness of corporate altruism. He contends that the resources available for such activities are very limited, and must come from discretionary funds available to management. Thus, charitable applications face competition from "luxurious office furnishings, attractive co-workers, company jets, lavish expense accounts and similar perquisites." "Socially responsible" outlays are made largely as the result of the desire of corporate executives to enjoy "the prestige and prominence that come from claiming to be 'corporate statesmen'" or to remove "discomforting external pressure" for corporate good works. "In other words," says Professor Manne, "the satisfaction or utility . . . come[s] from being seen to make the expenditure and not from the results allegedly purchased," leading to ineffective programs at best and socially harmful efforts at worst.

Dr. Manne concludes that his examination of the impact of "voluntary, independent corporate action" raises serious doubts as to whether such action produces any increase in social welfare. He finds his doubts confirmed by "the numerous advocates of the doctrine of corporate social responsibility who would...allow industry...to avoid competitive solutions." He sees in this a curious paradox: The doctrine of corporate social responsibility, "offered by many as a scheme to popularize and protect free enterprise, can only succeed if the free market is abandoned in favor of greater government controls."

Professor Wallich, Seymour H. Knox professor of economics at Yale University, takes a very different tack. Dr. Wallich believes that corporate social responsibility has the advantage of "shifting from the public to the private sector activities that should be performed with maximum economy rather than maximum bureaucracy. It fits into the design of a pluralistic society seeking a high degree of decentralization."

He defines corporate social responsibility in broad terms, saying, "I take 'responsibility' to mean a condition in which the corporation is at least in some measure a free agent," and he contends that the case for socially responsible corporate activity is supported by what he calls "functional considerations." Admitting that he is over-simplifying somewhat, Dr. Wallich says our society has two sets of objectives: "the production of goods and services at minimum cost, and...the protection of the environment and the achievement of social equity." There are, he says, two sets of instruments to achieve these ends: government and corporations. Each has unique responsibilities, but there is a wide range of activities in which the two working together—or at least in complementary ways—can bring about the best results.

Another "functional consideration," he states, involves the "possible advantages accruing to corporations, to their executives and stockholders, and perhaps to society," as the result of social programs carried out by corporations and funded by higher prices.

The exercise of corporate responsibility, according to Dr. Wallich, involves three basic elements: setting objectives, deciding whether or not to pursue given objectives, and financing such objectives. Such business decision making is "severely constrained by the law and the market." No single corporation in a competitive industry can afford the extra costs—and the resultant higher prices for its products—that, for example, an extensive pollution control program would impose. It would price itself out of the market. If, to avoid competitive extinction, the various corporations of a given industry enter into a cooperative agreement which results in

doctrine of corporate social responsibility who would...allow industry...to avoid competitive solutions." He sees in this a curious paradox: The doctrine of corporate social responsibility, "offered by many as a scheme to popularize and protect free enterprise, can only succeed if the free market is abandoned in favor of greater government controls."

Professor Wallich, Seymour H. Knox professor of economics at Yale University, takes a very different tack. Dr. Wallich believes that corporate social responsibility has the advantage of "shifting from the public to the private sector activities that should be performed with maximum economy rather than maximum bureaucracy. It fits into the design of a pluralistic society seeking a high degree of decentralization."

He defines corporate social responsibility in broad terms, saying, "I take 'responsibility' to mean a condition in which the corporation is at least in some measure a free agent," and he contends that the case for socially responsible corporate activity is supported by what he calls "functional considerations." Admitting that he is over-simplifying somewhat, Dr. Wallich says our society has two sets of objectives: "the production of goods and services at minimum cost, and...the protection of the environment and the achievement of social equity." There are, he says, two sets of instruments to achieve these ends: government and corporations. Each has unique responsibilities, but there is a wide range of activities in which the two working together—or at least in complementary ways—can bring about the best results.

Another "functional consideration," he states, involves the "possible advantages accruing to corporations, to their executives and stockholders, and perhaps to society," as the result of social programs carried out by corporations and funded by higher prices.

The exercise of corporate responsibility, according to Dr. Wallich, involves three basic elements: setting objectives, deciding whether or not to pursue given objectives, and financing such objectives. Such business decision making is "severely constrained by the law and the market." No single corporation in a competitive industry can afford the extra costs—and the resultant higher prices for its products—that, for example, an extensive pollution control program would impose. It would price itself out of the market. If, to avoid competitive extinction, the various corporations of a given industry enter into a cooperative agreement which results in higher prices, they would probably find themselves stymied by anti-trust laws. Under these circumstances, "corporations may discharge their responsibility" by requesting "government to tax or otherwise regulate them," or by seeking modifications in antitrust policy to permit socially responsible corporate cooperation, according to Dr. Wallich.

Turning to the advantages that might yield for corporations and their officers and stockholders from social programs, Dr. Wallich considers the impact of modern corporate continuity. The modern corporation does not fit the textbook model of a firm which "produces a product over whose demand it has no control" and which "closes up shop" when the demand disappears. Today, "the ordinary unregulated firm...seeks continuity" through product diversification. This concern with continuity causes "the interests of the corporation [to] become more oriented toward the long-run. Short-run profit maximization may be harmful to long-term survival." Thus, "recognition of social responsibilities may give the corporation the kind of acceptance in the community that it needs if it plans to be an ongoing operation."

"Recognition that the stockholder with a diversified portfo. has a broader range of interests than the maximization of the prof of any one corporation" is another factor favoring corporate soc activity, says Professor Wallich. For example, one company mig... conduct a training program for unskilled labor, and some of the trainees might leave to work for a competitor. The first firm would get no return from the investment whereas its competitor would. The diversified stockholder, if he holds stock in both firms, "will get his return from one firm or the other. The first firm would deprive the stockholder of a feasible return if it failed to make the investment in training, regardless of whether it or the competitor reaps ti benefits."

Dr. Wallich favors "stockholder instructions to the corpo. tion...to make corporations properly responsible to stockhold interest." He sees "a careful and reasonable activation of the potential power of the stockholder"—the "large institutional investors, in particular"—as the most effective means of inducing this response. And, in concluding, he believes that stockholder activism "augurs well for the adaptability of the corporate system to a more demanding world."

FOREWORD

Today, with the growing concern over the deterioration of our natural and social environments, we hear frequent and often vehement calls for socially responsible corporate action.

Just what is corporate social responsibility? There seems to be no simple answer. The phrase is used by advocates of a great variety of often conflicting programs and policies. Some contend that corporations have social responsibilities in a wide range of fields, many of them only remotely connected with business functions. Others hold that corporate sponsibility extends at least to the direct social and environmental impact of business activity. Still others argue that usiness enterprises have as their sole responsibility the maximization of their stockholders' profits.

In this debate, Professors Manne and Wallich consider these and other views of corporate social responsibility from an economic standpoint. They come to different conclusions but, in the process, this complex and important issue is further illuminated. As its twenty-third Rational Debate, the American Enterprise Institute is pleased to present this stimulating discussion of a major subject of public policy.

November 1972

William J. Baroody
President
American Enterprise Institute
for Public Policy Research

CONTENTS

FIRST LECTURE

HENRY G. MANNE

Introduction

The concept of corporate social responsibility, for all its popularity today, has not had a distinguished intellectual history in America. The idea has never been integrated in any systematic manner into either traditional or more contemporary modes of economic theory. In one sense, as we shall see, the idea can be subsumed as part of the broader subject of the economics of charity, on which a serious literature has recently begun to develop. But this newer theory about charity still cannot tell us much about corporate behavior, and the task before us is to analyze the concept of corporate social activity as a part of an integrated theory of corporations.

The poor scholarly heritage of corporate social responsibility cannot hide the popularity of the idea. Since its modern introduction in the early 1930s as an effort to counteract public hostility towards business, the idea has enjoyed periodic and substantial vogue in the business world. Academics, until recently, have not been overly sympathetic. The idea was alluded to by Berle and Means in *The Modern Corporation and Private Property* in 1932, and received its next, and fuller, academic consideration in 1954 in Berle's *The 20th Century Capitalist Revolution.*

From the thirties to the present there has been a continuing discussion in popular journals and magazines about the matter. And the outpouring of claims by businessmen, that

1

they observe social and not selfish goals, continues unabated, even though they show little ability to agree on just what the special responsibilities of corporations may be. Of course during World War II, in this country as in Germany, corporations loudly proclaimed the principal goal to be winning the war, not making a profit. In the early postwar era, at one time or another, such disparate notions as aesthetic industrial architecture, scholarships for the needy, support of private universities, sponsorship of art museums and symphony orchestras, and old stand-bys like the Community Chest, Boy Scouts and local hospitals headed the corporate popularity list. In the late 1950s, in keeping with the nation's increased attention to racial matters, advocates of corporate social responsibility turned their attention to increased hiring of Black workers and job training programs for the unskilled.

The more recent history of corporate social responsibility has continued to follow the social and economic concerns of the broader public. As product and then job safety became popular concerns in the 1960s, advocates of corporate social responsibility championed safer products, increased quality controls, and the installation of safer work equipment, as social responsibilities of business. As the nation began to face increasingly critical problems of inflation and an unfavorable balance of trade, advocates of corporate social responsibility urged voluntary restraints on prices, on imports of goods and on the export of capital. Most recently, as the ecology issue has accelerated into greater prominence, the focus for proponents of voluntary corporate social activity has been on various aspects of air and water pollution, especially

automobile and factory emissions and the use of public water-ways for waste disposal.

There have been numerous minor proposals as well, like preferential hiring for females, the cessation of production in unpopular countries—notably South Africa—and the end of production of particular products, such as napalm and leaded fuels.

This then is a brief history and catalog of some of the more prominent features of the concept of corporate social responsibility. Such a listing gives little of the true flavor or the real economic or social significance of this concept. It tells us nothing about either the sources of the demands made nor of the possible alternative motivations of advocates of corporate social responsibility. Most important of all, it tells us nothing about the economic implications of this doctrine: the feasibility of corporate altruism, the likelihood that corporate decision makers would make unselfish decisions, and the possibility that voluntary action can really accomplish its announced goals.

Definition of Corporate Social Responsibility

First, however, it would serve the cause of logic to have a clear definition of corporate social responsibility. For advocates of particular projects, this has never been a matter of any concern, since they have simply been asserting their own desire for certain results. Thus they have not felt constrained to define terms or to try to develop a consistent theory of corporate social behavior. There is, as we shall see, a consider-

able amount of confusion inherent in the common use of the phrase "corporate social responsibility."

Any working definition of the idea of corporate social responsibility must begin with the idea that the expenditure or activity be one for which the marginal returns to the corporation are less than the returns available from some alternative expenditure. That is not to say that the company must in absolute terms lose money but simply that it makes less money than would otherwise be the case. Without this feature as a starting point we are left with nothing significantly different from Adam Smith's unseen hand, which, by virtue of selfish individual behavior, guides all economic resources to their socially optimal use.

Many apologists for the social responsibility idea, particularly business spokesmen, are unwilling to admit this "non-business" motivation and preclude the logic of their own positions by proclaiming that the notion is really one of enlightened self-interest or long-run profit maximization. But selection of the relevant time span for corporate planning is *par excellence* a managerial function, and these statements are defending either corporate social action or profit maximization, but not both as they claim.

Ralph Nader illustrates this contradiction when he claims that what he advocates corporations doing voluntarily would constitute the most profitable course for the company. But if this argument is being seriously advanced, then the only argument is about who should have the power to make the managerial decisions for the company, the officers and directors, or Ralph Nader. But this is merely rhetoric on Nader's part, as he certainly does advocate voluntary corporate action

that would in fact not be in the shareholders' economic interests, in the long run or the short run.

Another aspect of any workable definition of corporate social responsibility is that the behavior of the firms must be voluntary. Thus there can be no law mandating the particular action that would otherwise look like social activity on the part of the corporation. And thus a nondiscriminatory hiring policy adopted by a corporation after the enactment of the Federal Civil Rights Act of 1968 could not represent corporate social responsibility, since the element of coercion would always be present or threatened. This is so even though an identical program voluntarily adopted by a corporation prior to that act might well have constituted voluntary altruistic behavior.

Government is not the only coercive force that may influence corporate behavior and thus prevent specific behavior's being denoted as socially responsible. For instance, a boycott by consumers, employees, or suppliers of materials would also establish this condition. If purportedly social behavior results from a successful boycott, threatened or actual, it must be assumed that the prescribed behavior was a profit-maximizing expenditure to avoid incurring more severe costs. The threat of a boycott is especially frightening to a consumer-oriented firm or industry, like soft drinks, supermarkets or canners, for which even a small percentage decline in customers may have devastating consequences. This would also be true of industries where close political ties may be necessary for survival, as is true of most regulated utilities or of licensed television stations.

Perusal of the industries claiming most frequently to have voluntarily modified their behavior in the interest of the public's safety or welfare strongly confirms this notion. One hears little public advocacy of corporate responsibility from the manufacturers of machine tools or heavy road building equipment.

Some other proposals for corporate behavior that do not fit our definition have in recent years been included in discussions of corporate social responsibility. These various proposals are for the "restructuring" of large corporations or for redefining their relationship to the federal government. Under the first category fall such proposals as those for "public" representation on boards of directors, or for special "public committees," or for constituent interest representation on boards of directors. The latter, for example, was proposed by Campaign GM 1971, with auto dealers, employees and consumers to be represented on the board. Increasingly, too, we find advocacy of greater government control over corporate decision-making machinery or for some form of government-business partnership.

None of these ideas is consistent with the definition of corporate social activity being discussed in this paper. They lack both the elements of voluntarism and charitable intent. Even though the public may frequently confuse almost anything proposed for large business enterprise today with the concept of corporate social responsibility, the economic analysis of true corporate altruism must necessarily differ from an analysis of these other proposals.

Still another part of the definition of corporate social responsibility is that the activity must be that of a corporation,

not that of an individual. Meaningful "corporate" social behavior must connote something different from individual contributions being made through a corporate conduit.

The corporate conduit for charitable contributions is quite common, especially since there are special tax advantages for an individual who wishes to give a certain amount of money to a tax exempt organization. Since the contribution is deductible to the corporation, no tax is ever paid on the earnings used in funding the gift. On the other hand if the corporation pays a dividend to the shareholder who makes his own contribution directly, the corporation must pay tax on the full earnings since no deduction is allowed for the dividend distribution to the shareholders. The shareholder has both income and a deduction, and thus realizes no special advantage as he would by using a corporation to make his contributions.

If we are to define away gifts made by corporations, all of whose shareholders are simply using it as a tax-saving conduit for their own giving, we are led to a strange paradox. We can only denote as corporate charity corporate expenditures that do not have the approval of all shareholders. And even some of these gifts may not represent unalloyed corporate charity, since the controlling shareholders may be utilizing a conduit scheme for themselves at some expense to the dissenting shareholders.

Presumably the clearest case of corporate altruism under this element of the definition would be one in which the managers of the corporation owned no shares and made contributions which all the shareholders would vote against. The possibility of true corporate altruism increases with the diffusion of stock ownership, since the latter circumstance would normally imply a lessened shareholder preference for the particular altruistic transaction. This, as we shall see, however, is not the end of the story.

The most difficult problem in talking about corporate social responsibility relates to the practical problem of classification of conduct. In practice it is often extremely difficult, if not impossible, to distinguish a purely business expenditure only alleged to have been made for the public's good from one actually made with real charitable intent. And, obviously, intents may be mixed in any one transaction. Furthermore, identical expenditures might at one moment be profit-maximizing and at another serve exactly the opposite purpose. We simply have no test that will allow us to distinguish the contribution made to the Community Chest in order to buy community goodwill from the contribution made by the true Samaritan.

Probably the most significant result of this confusion is the belief on the part of scholars and the public that corporations are considerably more charitable than, in fact, they are. We can only hope that in time methods of measurement will be developed so that better policy prescriptions can be offered.

The Advocates of Corporate Social Responsibility

Before examining the economic aspects of the question of corporate social responsibility, it might be well to put the issue in perspective by noticing which groups in our society advocate nonprofit behavior for corporations and to offer some hypotheses about the motivation of these individuals.

Government officials are maximizers just as much as investors or industrialists are, and their own utility is generally served by increases in governmental power. The concept of corporate social responsibility suits them almost perfectly. Today, as in years gone by, much new legislation is vaunted as making business more responsible to the public and as controlling the venal instincts of capitalists. But in fact our political system is such that these regulatory provisions are often highly beneficial to the politicians while carrying a large price tag for the public.

It is easy for politicians to take credit for vanquishing polluters while making no disclosure to the public of how much the cleanliness will cost them. And if for these and other governmental reasons prices rise, then we find politicians adopting price control laws to insure socially responsible behavior by the corporations. The concept of corporate social responsibility is truly ideal for government officials who wish to claim credit for all public benefits and accept no responsibility for increased costs and long-run antisocial effects.

American intellectuals of the left have also found happy hunting in the realm of corporate social responsibility. From Veblen and Ripley to Berle, Galbraith and Nader, we have long been treated to one strained explanation after another of why free markets are not good for us. The alleged assumptions of the free market model are derided; the myth of growing monopoly is constantly repeated; and the free market's inability to cope with certain externalities and social problems is blown out of all proportion.

The idea of corporate social responsibility fits all the liberal intellectual's predilections. It makes a moral issue out of business behavior; it accentuates the monopoly issue, since without some monopoly power, nonprofit oriented behavior seems unlikely; and it fits snugly with the recently discovered ecological crisis. The idea of corporate social responsibility becomes a convenient peg on which to hang every hackneyed criticism of business conduct and even a few new ones, like the lack of democracy and due process in dealing with employees, customers or the community. But we are still awaiting the serious intellectual defense of all this.

But probably the most important group to enthuse about corporate social responsibility is businessmen themselves, particularly executives of larger corporations. There would seem to be several explanations for this phenomenon. First, businessmen as a group are at best only slightly more expert in economic theory than the general population. And, like others, they may espouse popular ideologies regardless of the underlying implications—even for their own behavior.

The concept of corporate responsibility flatters businessmen that they are the divine-elect, as Andrew Carnegie would have had it. They are not merely responsible for producing diaper pins or corrugated sheet metal or rock crushers, but they are obliged to look after us lesser beings as well. It is thus easy for some businessmen to believe that universities would collapse, the air become unbreathable, and civilization be lost if they did not do good according to the gospel of business statesmanship.

But business advocacy of corporate responsibility is not principally a matter of ideology or psychology. It is economic.

Corporate responsibility is good business because it is good public relations. Certainly in the economic propaganda war that has been waged for so long now, business would be ill-advised to let politicians and consumerists claim all the credit for taming the corporate beasts—at least so long as the voting public thinks that corporations are beasts that must be tamed. One has only to look at the public pronouncements of General Motors since the Nader-inspired Project on Corporate Responsibility began its Campaign GM. Parts of their annual report now read like chapters from a corporate activist's text, implying that management operates the company as a public service institution devoted to improvements in social welfare but not in profits.

For good public relations reasons, and for other reasons we shall examine below, corporations will continue their efforts to buy political and social goodwill by asserting non-capitalistic values. One of the great ironies about this whole issue is that no individual firm can profit from voluntarily advocating the traditional values and ethics of the free enterprise system, no matter how strong a case can be made for it. Gain, at least in the public relations area, comes only from promising something for nothing.

The late Joseph Schumpeter argued, in his *Capitalism, Socialism and Democracy,* that as corporations grew and became bureaucratized, business executives would cease to think and act like entrepreneurs and would, therefore, cease to defend capitalism. Schumpeter may have been correct for the wrong reason. Contrary to his view, businessmen still behave precisely as the utility maximizers classical economic theory described. But today's maximizing behavior includes

11

advocating the non-maximization of profits. So, it is true that businessmen have largely ceased to defend business, but only because that was the businesslike thing to do.

Economic Aspects

It remains then to look seriously at some of the economic issues implicit in the concept of corporate social responsibility. Unfortunately we can only conjecture about most of the problems, since the hard data necessary for clear resolutions is totally lacking. Nonetheless it should be helpful to have some sort of economic model to show, at least a priori, the parameters of corporate social responsibility and to point up what the real questions in the area are.

The first and by all odds the most important question to ask is whether behavior that can be denoted as corporate social activity is in any significant sense feasible. That is, is it reasonable to assume that corporations really engage in social activity just because the managers say that that is what they are doing? Next, assuming that some amount of corporate social behavior is feasible, is it likely that corporate managers will use discretionary corporate funds for socially responsible purposes rather than for their own personal ends? And even if we can anticipate some social behavior on their part, should we anticipate much or little? Finally, assuming the feasibility of significant corporate giving and the likelihood of managers actually using discretionary funds in this manner, is there any reason to assume that their behavior will actually serve the announced social goal?

In addressing the first question of the feasibility of corporate social behavior, we must note that if the industry involved is one approaching the limits of the perfect competition model, no producer will be able voluntarily to increase his own costs and survive if his competitors do not act in the same way. Such an increase in cost would simply result in this now "less efficient" producer's not surviving, though the actual speed and form of exit from the industry may vary depending on different factors.

In the real world, however, some firms are more efficient producers than others and have lower short-run marginal costs than others. These firms produce profits for themselves by selling at a price which is in excess of their marginal cost. These profits may represent gains from specialized assets that may be people, ideas, land or a patent. But in the broadest sense they are defined or constrained by the long-run costs necessary to duplicate those specialized resources or to attract other assets to the higher productivity use.

This differential represents profits, since all other revenue simply covers the competitive replacement price of factor inputs. Probably, as a truly long-run phenomenon, the source of these profits cannot persist without some special grant of power or governmentally protected monopoly position, since new entrants or new productive equipment will tend to compete the profit away. Nonetheless, for present purposes it is sufficient to note that rents or profit do occur as a result of government policy, or as a result of the differences in foresight common in a world of uncertainty.

The more profitable firms will be able to use those profits for the higher costs implied by voluntary corporate altruism and still survive, though even this additional cost may lead them to produce less and earn less profit. The size of the effects will vary with circumstances, but the direction of the effect will be as stated.[1]

Shareholders will generally treat any corporate expenditure that reduces their wealth position with disfavor regardless of the purpose for which the expenditure was made. Any non-wealth maximizing expenditure will be seen as a reduction of the residual that could otherwise be claimed by shareholders. Thus as managers are seen to be expending corporate resources in a non-remunerative fashion, that corporation will have to pay more for its capital in the future.

This holds true even though the firm was previously realizing monopoly profits. No matter how high the corporation's earnings, the price per share will adjust so that the per share return is still only the competitive rate of return on the market value. If the anticipated return is diminished by "social" expenditures, the price of a share will decline until it provides the market rate of return on investments of the same quality.

Thus the cost of the "social" expenditure will be visited on those who held the shares at the time information about the anticipated expenditures was reflected in the share price. Since any future rents or profits were fully capitalized into the present wealth of those who held the shares at the time the higher earnings were originally anticipated, there is, for a shareholder, no costless way to use corporate resources for social purposes, even if the firm is not bankrupted by the expenditure. The firm will be worth less; and in the longer run it will have to pay more for its capital in order to continue to offer its new nonprofit venture. Survival could also be postulated on the basis of consumer willingness to purchase the same quantity of the firm's output at a higher price, but this would not seem as likely as the effect on shareholders.

But describing those firms which can theoretically survive nonwealth-maximizing expenditures is just a starting point. Even if managers of less than perfectly competitive firms wished to behave in this fashion, there are still significant barriers to their doing so.

Investors effect managerial discretion in ways other than by reducing their willingness to invest for lower returns; they also play an important role in displacing incumbent control groups.

While there is little of this effect where 51 percent or more of a company's stock is held by one person (or by a controlling group acting as one person), diffusion of enough shares to allow a control block to be formed makes possible the functioning of an effective market for corporate control. In such companies the incentive to purchase control will be measured by the difference between the current price of shares and the price that can be anticipated with more efficient or less "charitable" managers.

This market for corporate control operates through the familiar devices of proxy fights, tender offers and mergers, each of which involves different costs, as well as different legal and strategic considerations. A fourth possibility, the direct sale by one individual or group of a controlling block of shares, is quite common in smaller or closely controlled corporations and may occasionally occur in larger companies as well. The premium paid for control is then included in the price of the block of shares purchased. Of course, managers may at any time be displaced by those presently in control of a corporation. But this really has no more implication for the issue of corporate behavior than any other case in which less efficient assets are displaced by more efficient ones.

If a direct sale of a control block of shares can be negotiated, in all likelihood the relative transaction costs to effectuate the new management arrangement will not be great. The new controlling shareholder or shareholders will simply elect new officers. More often, however, incumbent controllers will not voluntarily relinquish their position, since they will normally not be able to claim the market value of control for themselves. Then one of the less voluntary forms of displacement has to be used. The costs of these displacement mechanisms have great significance for the matter of corporate responsibility.

An outside group trying to take over control of a corporation must assume that it can operate the corporation more profitably than the incumbents and realize a gain in the price of the company's shares when their greater ability is capitalized into the market price of the stock.[2] And they must also assume that the gain they will realize will be greater than the costs they incur in acquiring control. That is, no one would voluntarily try to take over control of a corporation in which he could not gain more than the cost of the takeover.

Thus to the extent that incumbent controllers by their managerial efficiency present no opportunity for outsiders to realize capital gains in excess of the displacement costs, they are safe from displacement through any of these capital market mechanisms. If for instance the costs of a successful proxy fight are assumed to be $2 million, then outsiders must believe that the appreciation in value of *their* stock holdings resulting from more efficient management will exceed that figure; otherwise they will not start a proxy fight. If no group believes that they can increase the value of their holdings by more than that amount, they will have no incentive to engage in a fight for control of this corporation. And more important, the incumbent managers will have discretionary use of up to two-million-minus-one dollars with little fear of displacement because these funds are not used for the shareholders.

As managers become more and more wasteful or charitable or even larcenous, the cost of a successful takeover declines, regardless of the mechanism used. For example, with a tender offer, the lower the price outsiders have to offer (whether in the form of cash or shares in another corporation), the more likely they are to try to purchase control through this device. The principal transaction costs (those over and above the purchase price for the shares in the poorly run company) are those for communicating the offer to the public and to brokers, filing and otherwise complying with S.E.C. rules under the Williams Act, expenses for an escrow arrangement and transfer agent, actual or imputed interest on money used to purchase the necessary number of shares, normal legal fees, commission, and probably litigation expenses.

In the case of a proxy fight, these costs will be supplemented by the substantial expenses necessary to prepare and mail out proxy solicitation materials to shareholders.

These are usually in addition to most of the types of expenses incurred to make a tender offer, and thus normally the tender offer is the less expensive of the two devices. But ultimately some number of shares must be purchased before any gains can be realized through a tender-offer takeover, while the proxy fight is a device for securing votes without incurring all the expenses required to purchase the larger number of shares. It might be anticipated that the proxy fight would be used more frequently in the case of control fights for large, profitable corporations, since these two factors would tend to make the cost of successfully acquiring an adequate number of shares through a tender offer very high. Nonetheless, as a general rule, we should expect, and do find, far fewer proxy fights than tender offers or mergers.

If there were no transaction costs in the operation of the market for corporate control, no manager who did not himself own sufficient shares to control a corporation could ever use corporate funds for nonprofitable social purposes. As soon as it became evident to shareholders that the price of their shares would appreciate if a less charitably inclined control group operated the corporation, one could fairly safely posit that the displacement would occur. Indeed, then the situation would be identical to that in which the owner of a corporation who did not personally manage it simply fired the less efficient employed manager in order to hire a known better one. We could not then assume the feasibility of any corporate charity.

But transaction costs do exist. It might be added parenthetically that it is not in the nature of the economic system that a great variety of legal barriers will exist, such as the

Williams Act, the S.E.C.'s Proxy Solicitation Rules and provisions dealing with management displacement in various regulated industries like banking and insurance. It is strange, yet not illogical, that these restrictive regulations protect inefficient incumbents against competition and thereby increase the funds available for so-called corporate social activities.

We have now seen two points affecting the economics of corporate social activity. In the first place, the amount expendable on these purposes, or for that matter any nonprofit purpose, is limited by the extent to which the market price for any firm's product exceeds its production cost.

The second factor is the existence of transaction costs for the displacement of managers. Existing managers can, within certain limits to be described below, use for their own purposes any rents produced by the corporation up to the amount that it would cost to displace them from their positions. That is, they must never waste, steal, or give away in total more than the amount others would pay to displace them.

It must be remembered, however, that the funds that can be safely used by managers for nonprofit activities are realized on an annual basis, while the displacement figure is a present value. Thus, if we assume a company with management displacement costs of $25 million and even larger rents, the maximum amount available each year for social purposes, assuming a discount rate of 10 percent, will be around $2.5 million. If the annual rents are less than that, then that will be the limiting figure. We can never conclude a priori that either of these limits will be zero, but it is also unlikely that, even for the largest companies, they will approach the scale necessary for programs regularly urged on corporations and

instituted by them under the rubric of corporate social responsibility.

The Likelihood that Discretionary Funds Will Be Used for Social Purposes

But just because we can describe the economic maxima for voluntary corporate altruism does not mean that the available funds will be used for such purposes. There is considerable discretion on the part of corporate managers about how the funds set by the two limits described above will be used, and there can be no presumption that they would be used for social rather than selfish purposes by incumbent managers. Rather, if these funds are truly discretionary and cannot be captured by shareholders, it would seem more reasonable to anticipate that the managers would claim them in the form of higher salaries, less work or other utility producing perquisites, especially those on which no income tax must be paid. The latter might include such things as lavish executive dining rooms, company jets, business meetings in attractive locations, and many other items of a similar nature.

Can we then ever expect managers to use any of these purely discretionary funds for purposes consistent with the corporate social responsibility idea? For a variety of reasons the answer would seem to be in the affirmative. Certainly of considerable importance is the fact that individuals do receive some pleasure or reward from delegating wealth to others for purposes the donor selects. We witness this behavior commonly, and thus we should anticipate corporate managers utilizing the available funds for charitable purposes in about

the same way that any wealthy individuals might be expected to contribute to charities, that is, to about the same extent that individuals with comparable personal wealth use it for charitable purposes.

It should be noted that the claim is not that it costs corporate controllers nothing to give away these funds, but rather that it costs them no more than it would if they were giving away their own funds. As in any exchange transaction the cost is simply the opportunity cost represented by the utility foregone from the next best alternative. As we shall see, however, there are some special, discernible factors operating on corporate executives that suggest a somewhat higher preference for corporate giving than for individual giving, all other things being equal.

There will be some dilution of normal donor benefits as a result of the fact that the corporation rather than the individual receives some of the credit for making the gift. Presumably there is some positive utility, if charity pleases a donor at all, from giving one's own funds rather than from merely directing the use of funds not so clearly owned by the person making the decision. However, one can also suppose a model for charity in which exactly the opposite would be true. In this model the entire gift would represent a cost and the benefits would come exclusively from the receipt of some value from either the beneficiary or someone else. This is a straight "purchase" model, and to use someone else's money to gain the same benefits would obviously be more desirable. This latter model may be the more realistic one to use in considering corporate social activity, though there are probably elements of both involved.

Clearly the direct gains to be had from corporate contributions that are not disguised business expenditures inure to the benefit of the decision makers and not the corporations. It is the individuals, not the corporation, who are asked to join prestigious boards of trustees or become directors of socially prominent groups. But at the same time we must remember that the gift does represent a cost to the individuals, since we have assumed heretofore that the funds could be used for personal gain.

There is no a priori reason to expect executives to give away a very substantial amount of funds that they could claim for themselves. And we have assumed that there is no market mechanism that could operate to shift these funds to shareholders or other potential claimants. The important point is that the funds necessary for corporate social responsibility would not really come from the corporation or shareholders at all. Rather, they have to come from the managers. Only social expenditures in excess of transaction costs could represent a reallocation of funds from shareholders to so-called socially responsible activities, and, as we have seen, there is little reason to anticipate much of that.

We can probably safely conclude that individuals with discretionary funds will utilize some of them for charitable purposes. This is a universal phenomenon, and there is no reason to doubt that the same will not be true in this case of allocation of discretionary funds just because the "legal title" to the funds does not lie with the allocator. However, we are still faced with considerable uncertainty about the amounts that would be involved. If the pattern of individual private charity were followed, the figures would fall in the

range of 3 percent of the discretionary funds.[3] Even if we assume these transaction-cost imposed limits to be substantial, it is still hard to believe that even for the largest corporation they would ever exceed $50 million present value, or $5 million per year discounting at 10 percent. This is a rough, but probably high guess, since the largest previously reported expenditure in a control fight was $4.5 million. But 3 percent of $5 million suggests a maximum voluntary use of discretionary funds for nonbusiness, corporate social purposes of only $150,000 per year for a very large corporation, and certainly less for others. Clearly we must look elsewhere if we are to take seriously the arguments for significant corporate social behavior.

There are some other factors that could significantly increase management's willingness to use discretionary funds for corporate social activity. Not the least of these factors is the difficulty that managers of very large corporations have in concealing extremely high compensation paid to themselves. If high personal compensation, say over $1 million a year for many executives, is known by shareholders, it is probably safe to conclude that some shareholder disaffection will set in. The effect of this information could be to lower the costs necessary to displace the managers. This idea can be observed commonly in most proxy fights. Those attempting to take over control often use a considerable portion of their proxy materials to allege that exorbitant compensation is being received by the incumbent managers. Furthermore, they promise to lower the direct compensation that they will take from the company (and undoubtedly do so, if successful in the fight). These are some additional market constraints that may limit the amount of discretionary funds the managers may be able to direct to themselves.

More important than the problem of shareholder disaffection is the possibility of some government response to the news of what sounds like very high management compensation figures. Certainly this has now become explicitly so with the existence of federal wage and price controls. But even apart from these controls, there has always been some danger of government intervention in the matter of high-sounding executive compensation. Undoubtedly, both greater concealment and lower payments have resulted from this pervasive fear. And manifestly any form of concealment indicates some lowering of the actual utility enjoyed by the executive, since what would have been the most preferred form of compensation is foregone.

The matter of concealment of receipt of discretionary funds is somewhat complicated and more often discussed in the tax literature than in that dealing with corporate charity.

In a sense the executive is faced with a trade-off between enjoyment of the funds and security. Maximum wealth utility would come from paying himself the entire amount of available discretionary funds. However, this alternative also presents him with maximum danger to his position.

At the other extreme, he can receive maximum security against capital market displacement mechanisms by distributing all the funds to shareholders. Indeed this may even raise displacement costs higher than they would otherwise be. But this alternative presents the executive with the lowest payoff in terms of his own utility preferences. Consequently he will try to choose from among various alternatives in between these two extremes. Some forms of compensation will allow easy concealment and still furnish fairly high utility. This could include such things as luxurious office furnishings, attractive co-workers, company jets, lavish expense accounts and similar perquisites of the job. The likelihood is high that these items would generally be chosen in preference to using the same funds for corporate social behavior.

Next we should consider the extent to which some of these discretionary funds will be "used up" in the form of leisure, or, as it would appear to an outside observer, as inefficiency in management. This may take the form of longer vacations, shorter work days, longer lunch hours, relaxed work habits or the like. Any of these again may allow a substantial enjoyment of benefits by the management with no significant additional risk of their displacement.

Finally, we must ask what positive utility, other than that previously referred to, would cause the allocator of discretionary funds to use some of them for corporate social purposes. Here some of the newer theories of the economics of charity may help us understand why executives may elect to use a significant portion of the available funds for purposes other than maximization of corporate profits.

Positive utility may be experienced by corporate executives either from the prestige and prominence that come from claiming to be "corporate statesmen," or it may come from removing some discomforting external pressure. Such pressures, coming either from one's business peers or from outside the business community, may create discomforts for corporate executives who do not conform to the standards demanded.

One need only notice the reams of literature published by business organizations like the Committee for Economic Development and by individual business spokesmen to realize that today the idea of corporate social responsibility is very popular in the business community. Previously an explanation was offered as to why this idea might be publicly urged by corporate executives; now we are looking at the effects that may flow from the existence of these statements. It should be noted that the two are not the same. The first dealt with motivation to make certain statements. The second deals with the motivation to make corporate gifts that stems from statements being made about corporate social behavior.

An illuminating illustration of the way in which this pressure is brought to bear on individual executives appears in the 1971 report of the Committee for Economic Development (CED): "Indiscriminate opposition to social change not only jeopardizes the interest of the single corporation, but also affects adversely the interest all corporations have in maintaining a climate conducive to the effective functioning of the entire business system." [4] Thus it is clear that the report is intended to further the kind of social pressure alluded to by arguing that each corporation or set of executives has an obligation, *in the interest of all corporations,* to further corporate social behavior.

It is also clear that pressures of this sort are designed to, and can, create a preference on the part of managers to conform to the prescribed standards. As the corporate responsibility idea becomes more popular with managers who have discretionary income (whether or not they are conscious of the economic nature of these funds), compliance with the idea will become one of the criteria by which businessmen judge each other in the business community. It is difficult to believe that individuals will not respond in some measure to this kind of pressure or that the size of their response will not be positively correlated with the intensity of the importuning. Clearly what can pass as corporate altruism must be near an all-time high today.

Outside pressures, too, play a role in the realization of the utility preferences of managers. If a contribution, program or activity will free the relevant corporate executive from pressure and harangue by outside groups, such as the Project on Corporate Responsibility, other Ralph Nader supported groups, or various environmental protection groups, this may well be the use of funds which has the highest utility for that individual. As we have already noted, expenditures of this sort present little danger of adverse governmental or shareholder reaction, and thus to the extent that some positive utility is realized by the executive, it is also effectively concealed.

This theory of "corporate" social activity has some other interesting implications. For one thing, since transaction costs in the market for corporate control create the most significant parameter for corporate social activity, we should anticipate more of such activity for those corporations where takeover costs are highest. Takeover costs are probably a function primarily of profitability and absolute size, and the degree of diffusion of share ownership will have an influence as well. Casual observation suggests that it is the leaders of so-called "Big Business" who are the most vocal and active supporters of the idea of corporate responsibility. It remains to be shown that this activity also correlates positively with profitability.

Another interesting implication of this theory of charitable giving is that it should make no great difference to the donor (realistically viewed as those in control of the corporation) whether or not the expenditures actually accomplish the purpose for which they are allegedly made. The important thing is that the contribution itself either gains the positive utility desired or relieves the donor of the disutility he is experiencing. In fact, as long as the contribution or activity is thought by its advocates to have the effect claimed for it, it will not be in the interest of the donor to expend any time or effort at all to find out what the actual result of the expenditure is. In other words, the satisfaction or utility will come from being seen to make the expenditure and not from the results allegedly purchased. Unsupervised and unattended "charity" may even do more social harm than good, and the danger that that will be the case is increased with the intensity of pressure for the alleged social expenditure.

An episode from recent history nicely illustrates this danger. In 1970 a group of so-called "Nader's Raiders" issued a widely publicized report on the working conditions of migrant orange pickers employed by the Minute Maid subsidiary of the Coca-Cola Corporation. (In fact the Coca-Cola Corporation was already engaged in efforts to alleviate some of the poor working conditions, but the appearance of the Nader report did accelerate these efforts.) This particular group of migrants were low-skilled workers who dwelled normally in the malarial swamps of Georgia and North and South Carolina. The move to the Florida orange groves certainly did not rid them of the illnesses they brought with them. Furthermore, they lived as best they could with little shelter, education for their children, medical care, or nourishing food, though in all likelihood conditions were even worse in the swamps. The correction program was aimed at alleviating these conditions and it is alleged to have cost the Coca-Cola Corporation several million dollars.

The corporation has taken well-publicized pride in its social accomplishments for these workers, and though they were unhappy that the Nader group ignored their previous voluntary efforts, there was really no disagreement about goals between Nader and Coke. But there was nothing said in Coca-Cola's press releases about certain other consequences that followed hard upon Coca-Cola's private scheme for social welfare.

The expenditure of additional funds for medical and other welfare purposes accelerated the introduction by Coca-Cola of automatic equipment used in orange picking. And for that reason the number of migrant workers employed by Coca-Cola diminished by about a third. No one ever asked whether those workers not employed, but who otherwise could have been, were made better or worse off by this private welfare program. When asked about their present whereabouts, a spokesman for the corporation replied with some anguished surprise in his voice, "I guess they've gone back to the swamps."

The important thing to notice is that no one, not Ralph Nader nor the Coca-Cola Corporation nor its executives, had any motivation to follow up on the real economic consequences of the program they adopted. We might consider the funds as having been spent on business public relations, or this may have been a use of discretionary funds to buy the executives' peace of mind. Whatever the case, the important thing is that there was no incentive to invest further funds to gain information on the effects of the expenditures.

Can Corporate Charity Gain Its Intended Goal?

This brings us to the final and perhaps most important question in the issue of corporate social responsibility: Can it be made to accomplish the ends claimed for it? Here it is hard to give even a qualified affirmative answer. In the first place, we have no definition of a social welfare function that is universally acceptable. This strongly suggests that any effort to maximize public good by private effort or otherwise is doomed to failure.

Furthermore, even within the limits of some broadly accepted goals, conflicts of a practical nature are bound to develop. The Coca-Cola situation illustrates one kind of problem, that of conflicts between competing employment groups. There are many other kinds of problems as well. Who is to say, for instance, that funds contributed to universities are better spent than funds utilized for pollution controls? What corporate executive can know with certainty that a decision not to locate a plant abroad in an effort to conserve domestic jobs does not do more harm to American consumers and investors than good to prospective employees?

To ask these questions is clearly to imply the answer: It is impossible to know in most instances that individual corporate altruism is not doing more harm than good, however measured. The difficulty is not one of lack of expertise by corporate executives. They may have or can easily acquire the most expert judgment available on the questions. But the ultimate problem, not limited to corporate charity by any means, still remains. It is not surprising that our previous analysis led us to the conclusion that most behavior called corporate social activity is likely either to be profit maximizing for the company or else designed to increase the utility of those in control of the company.

Another practical problem stems from the inability of companies acting individually to accomplish their stated goal. One clear illustration comes with the independent effort of one or more, but not all, companies along a river voluntarily to control pollution killing the fish population of the river. One uncooperative company may supply all the effluent necessary to kill all the fish, and, therefore, the additional costs to the socially minded corporations would have been incurred with no real benefit being realized at all. Other problems relate to research and development costs not shared by all the corporations that might benefit (the "free-rider" problem) and various economic policies in connection with international trade.

The most popular solution offered for dealing with these problems is for the concerned corporations to engage in some kind of cooperative effort. This argument quite logically implies adjustments in the federal antitrust laws, but it also implies something even more ominous.

Chapter five of the CED report on the social responsibilities of business corporations is entitled "A Government-Business Partnership for Social Progress." What is described there is fundamentally a system of central government planning, with the policy goals developed in discussion with the interested business corporations. Business and government would then presumably work together in "a constructive partnership for accelerating social progress."[5]

The report is quite clear in stating that this is not merely to be a case of government purchasing its needs in the private market. "Fundamentally, it offers a new means for developing the innate capabilities of political democracy and a private enterprise economy into a new political-economic system capable of managing social and technological change in the interest of a better social order."[6] These sentiments have been echoed recently in statements by former Secretary of the Treasury Connally.[7]

As one examines these statements they appear to be barely veiled demands for a shift away from the disciplines of full-fledged domestic and international competition towards a scheme of protectionism, cartelization and central planning. The claim that this will contribute to the social welfare is questionable at best and probably utterly deceptive. Yet few presumably sincere advocates of the concept of corporate social responsibility have noted this rather frightening implication of the doctrine. Indeed most have claimed its inherent compatibility with a free enterprise system. But the doctrine will not fit easily and neatly with our traditional views of competitive enterprise. Ultimately it is only consistent with a system that commands "cooperative behavior" from industries as one side of a "government-business partnership."

We have seen such partnerships before. Nazi Germany was probably the clearest example of private business and government engaging in a partnership for "social" ends. At the present moment the Japanese partnership seems limited largely to the matter of protecting Japanese trade interests, as allegedly would be former Secretary Connally's proposals. But once this kind of interdependence develops between government and business, government will ultimately be the dominant partner. And there is no safe way to predict the ends toward which that domination will be exercised. It is difficult to imagine a more sinister configuration for business and government than one in which government is responsible for the high profits and the good life of a series of large, cartelized industries.

Conclusion

We have come through a considerably complex analysis of what could be one of the dominant economic issues of our time. To many it has seemed simply a tempest in a teapot, since their instincts tell them that quantitatively the whole matter is not very important. Our own analysis suggests that the very fact that there is talk about corporate social responsibility may influence some people more than any charitable impulse. Nonetheless, even though significant empirical data are still lacking, we have developed a model which shows that in all likelihood there is room for some behavior that will generally be regarded as corporate social activity, though the motive for it may belie that characterization. Those with discretion over these funds have a positive interest in allocating them in this fashion, and we can safely assume that certain funds are being so expended. In all likelihood, this behavior is not as great as identical or similar activities done for more traditional business purposes, but its existence cannot be denied.

When we begin to examine the impact of this behavior, doubts develop as to whether any increase in social welfare can be assured by voluntary, independent corporate action. These doubts seem to be confirmed by the numerous advocates of the doctrine of corporate social responsibility who would therefore allow industry a greater degree of freedom to avoid competitive solutions, with or without the assistance of the government. At this point advocates of corporate social responsibility must face a disheartening paradox: corporate responsibility, a doctrine offered by many as a scheme to popularize and protect free enterprise, can only succeed if the free market is abandoned in favor of greater government controls. Surely the game is not worth the candle.

SECOND LECTURE

HENRY C. WALLICH

The Case for Social Responsibility of Corporations

Views about social responsibility of corporations have deep roots. The widespread belief that corporations have a special responsibility to society draws nourishment from the assertion that corporations are creatures of the state, originally created by act of the sovereign. The other side, which views corporations as instruments simply of their stockholders, rests its case on the origin of the corporation in contract. The acts of the state connected with incorporation have become routine, the powers expressed in charters are very broad, and owners choose between conducting their business in the form of a corporation or a partnership depending largely on tax considerations and the advantages of limited liability. The very term "corporation" is no longer descriptive of the uncorporeal shell that is being brought into the world, in contrast to the much apter Spanish term "sociedad anónima."

The ideological fronts are curiously inverted on this issue. The conservative side, usually willing to pay tribute to tradition and history, here leans on the abstract reasoning of the law of contract. The liberal side, usually no great admirer of the paraphernalia of the past, acknowledges a line of reasoning that has strong historical overtones. I shall try to steer clear of both approaches, and base my case for the social responsibility of corporations on what seem to be functional considerations. Specifically, I shall argue that this case is supported by:

1. the analysis of the relationship between goals and instruments;

2. the theory of decision making under uncertainty;

3. the diversification prevailing in the portfolios of most stockholders, which makes stockholders' interest broader than their interest in any one corporation;

4. the continuing character of unregulated corporations today, which are no longer identified with the life cycle of any one product, but seek to become ongoing entities by updating their product-mix; and

5. possible advantages accruing to corporations, to their executives and stockholders, and perhaps to society, from carrying out social programs efficiently and financing them by raising prices, i.e., with the equivalent of a sales tax, as contrasted with similar programs conducted inefficiently by a centralized bureaucracy and financed with progressive income taxes.

Today the issue is sharpening. Pressure upon the environment and the demand for social betterment widens the area of economic policy where the market, at least as presently constituted, is not obviously the best solution. Some would say that for some of these objectives the market is a totally inappropriate solution. On the other hand, the use of the market as a guidance mechanism seems to encounter somewhat less ideological opposition, as indicated by the experience of socialist countries. Likewise, there seems to be a mounting receptivity to the use of public corporations as means of protecting certain business-type operations of governments, for instance the post office, against the anti-economic effects of the political process.

In any event, the issue is not whether the private corporation can or cannot legitimately be required by society to perform certain functions. In an age when the corporate income tax rate is 48 percent, it should be obvious that society can make corporations do anything it wants. The incidental fact that nobody knows, and nobody seems urgently interested to discover, who really pays these corporate taxes—stockholders, consumers, or workers—throws a peculiar light on efforts to be extremely precise about the rights and obligations of corporations in other respects. It is worth noting at this point that, thanks to the corporate tax and to the deductibility of charitable contributions (up to 5 percent of income) even when unrelated to business expenses, it is cheaper for the taxpayer to meet such "responsibilities" from corporate pretax income than from dividend income. This happens to be a peculiarity of the American tax system. It does not bear on the broader issue of corporate responsibility but it cannot be ignored as a practical consideration.

The Meaning of Corporate Responsibility

Corporations today are being asked to do a host of things. They are to turn out useful products, at a reasonable price, that give reliable service, do not damage the environment, and are easy to dispose of. In producing these goods and services, corporations are to treat their workers well, avoid discrimination, avoid pollution, conserve resources, pay taxes, and observe a variety of laws covering these and other matters. They are to contribute to society's goals in areas outside or only marginally related to their own business, such as education, urban renewal, and good government. In what sense, and under what conditions, can these inherently desirable objectives be considered "corporate responsibilities," and who or what makes them so?

I take "responsibility" to mean a condition in which the corporation is at least in some measure a free agent. To the extent that any of the foregoing social objectives are imposed upon the corporation by law, the corporation exercises no responsibility when it implements them. Even so, compliance with the law can be generous or niggardly; there are border-lines and grey areas where the corporation can make decisions and exercise responsibility.

In the areas of production, of relations with labor, suppliers, and customers, the corporation is under the control of the market. In a fundamental sense, it cannot freely determine the kind of product customers are to buy, or its price, or the wages to be paid. Again, there are ranges of discretion. The larger the corporation, the greater its freedom to vary product, price, and wages. Opinions differ as to the extent to which a corporation, by advertising, can condition its customers and achieve acceptance of socially undesirable products. Nevertheless, it seems clear, for instance, that an advanced-type car that met maximum safety and anti-pollution standards would not be a commercial success if it had to be sold in competition with ordinary cars at a price covering the extra costs. Neither could a corporation obtain labor at wage

rates substantially below what other firms in the same industry are paying.

It is frequently said that power implies responsibility. It is
then concluded that, because corporations are supposed to
have great power, they must be held accountable in a very
far-reaching sense. It is true, of course, that corporations take
actions that influence large numbers of people decisively.
These actions, however, do not imply a commensurate use of
power. Assuming the corporation wants to stay in business,
its action is severely constrained by the law and by the market.
Power exists only at the margin.

Three basic activities seem to be involved in the exercise
of corporate responsibility:

1. the setting of objectives,
2. the decision whether or not to pursue given objectives, and
3. the financing of these objectives.

For instance, the government may set a specific objective,
offer a reward to corporations pursuing it, and leave it up to
the corporation to accept the offer or not. This is exemplified
by a government decision to increase the rate of growth or
the competitiveness of American industry by means of an
investment tax credit. The responsibility of the corporation,
in accepting or rejecting, is a fairly narrow one. Alternatively,
the government may establish some kind of tax preference
for a much broader objective, say, research and development.
In that case, the corporation not only decides on acceptance
or rejection of the offer, but also chooses the goal of the
research. It exercises a much wider responsibility. In either

case, however, the financing comes from the government. As a third possibility, the corporation may freely decide to pursue some social purpose, and do so out of its own resources. It is in this area that most people find the core of responsible corporate action.

This enumeration shows that, in relation to the full range of corporate activities, the exercise of this kind of responsibility has fairly narrow limits. It shows also that, where there is a strong consensus that corporations should engage in certain activities, the most straightforward procedure is either to require them to do so by law, or to induce them through compensation, be it in the form of tax subsidies or penalties, or of an outside government contract. Corporate responsibilities that have not been backed by law or financial inducements may lack the support of a broad consensus, either as to the desirability of a goal or the moral obligation of corporations to pursue it.

To act in compliance with a law or in response to financing offered by government does not downgrade the importance of the action. On the contrary, the absence of a wide range of discretion and hence responsibility for the corporation is likely to be an index of the importance that society attaches to the activity. Government's decision to delegate the function to a corporation simply implies that the corporation appears to be the most appropriate instrumentality.

The corporation may have a comparative advantage in carrying out the activity, as contrasted with the government itself or some other agency, as for instance in on-the-job training. It may be the only candidate, as in building safety devices into products. Corporate intervention may be preferable on grounds of decentralization, of more economic or less political operation. Nevertheless, important as these activities may be, and desirable as the employment of corporations as instrumentalities of the government may be, I would not regard this range of activities as falling under the general heading of "corporate responsibility."

Areas of Responsibility

In order to give concreteness to the argument, it may be helpful to draw up a list of some of the major areas in which corporations are exercising responsibility or in which social critics have held them to have responsibilities. Obviously such a list is bound to be incomplete, and to contain activities of widely varying importance, both to the corporation and to society. Among these areas of responsibility are:

1. efficiency in the use of resources,
2. adequate expansion to provide growth of output and jobs,
3. research and development,
4. safe and economical product design,
5. socially desirable location of new plants,
6. protection of the environment,
7. conservation of resources,
8. employment and training of minority and handicapped labor,
9. civil rights and equal opportunity,
10. urban renewal,
11. medical care,
12. education, and
13. cultural pursuits.

The degree of responsibility for any of these social objectives depends, in the first place, on the amount of discretion that the law and the market offer to the corporation. It depends, second, on the comparative advantage that the corporation may have in dealing with any particular objective. And it depends, third, on how far the market falls short of meeting social objectives.

The question therefore is to what extent these objectives should be pursued by government action, left to the market, or left to corporate responsibility. None of these approaches precludes any of the others. Where the government takes the principal role, a subsidiary one may still remain for corporate responsibility. In some areas, the corporate contribution is bound to be marginal because the corporation has little to do with objectives such as education, medical care, and cultural pursuits. In evaluating the role of the market, the critical issue is not only "how perfect" it is in a technical sense. Externalities need to be considered. And even in their absence, the workings of the market may not be what society considers optimal, for instance with respect to the distribution of income. Through the political process, people may establish a hierarchy of values different from that which their market behavior brings about. To take another example, the valuation placed on the future may not be correctly expressed by the market rate of interest, which, employed as a discount factor, would make the world of our great-grandchildren worth a great deal less than we may intuitively believe it to be. Some comments on how to approach problems of this kind will be found in the concluding section of this paper.

One way in which corporations may discharge their responsibility is to request government to tax or otherwise regulate them when competition makes voluntary action impossible. The complementary case—a request for subsidization—stands in no special need of recommendation.

The questions posed here can be clarified by an examination in more technical terms, to which we now turn.

Targets and Instruments

The respective roles of government and of corporations in helping to attain society's objectives can be examined in terms of the familiar framework relating the number of targets to the number of instruments. At the expense of some abstraction, the community can be viewed as having two sets of objectives: (1) the production of goods and services at minimum costs, and (2) the protection of the environment and the achievement of social equity. The community has two instruments: (a) the government and (b) corporations. Both instruments affect the attainment of both targets, although each instrument affects each target in different degree. If the strength of the two instruments is known, this gives a simple system of two equations with two unknowns, the latter being the degree of target achievement. With two equations and two unknowns there is a solution.

A use frequently made of this framework envisages the existence of "dilemma situations." Such a dilemma exists when the pursuit of one objective does injury to the attainment of the other. For example, the effort to increase production may injure the environment and create social

45

inequities. The effort to protect the environment and establish social equity may hamper production. Under such circumstances, it becomes important to assign each respective objective the instrument that has a comparative advantage in attaining it. If we are prepared to assume that corporations have a comparative advantage in producing goods and services, and that government has a comparative advantage in protecting the environment and social equity, it would then be a mistake to let government look after production, and corporations after environment and equity. The reverse assignment will give superior results. That superior assignment is of course the way in which society has largely organized itself.

It would nevertheless be a mistake to conclude that their unquestioned comparative advantage entitles government or corporations to ignore the objective with respect to which they have a comparative disadvantage. The proponents of the corporate social responsibility believe that these relationships of goals and instruments are not immutable. The trade-off between the impact of corporations on production and on the environment and equity is not linear. Efforts to move in either direction are subject to diminishing returns. Given increases in production can only be bought at more rapidly mounting damage to environment and equity. On the other hand, corporate efforts to pursue environmental protection and equity, carried far enough, will result in losses to production at an increasing rate. The same changing trade-off can be traced on the government's side.

The function of social policy is precisely to guide government and corporate activity so that the comparative advantage of either vanishes. The activities of both must be shifted to the point where the two objectives have the same trade-off for government and corporations. The opponents of a corporate policy deliberately aimed at social objectives claim that corporations are beset by an immutable comparative disadvantage with respect to these objectives. Proponents, on the other hand, believe that the trade-off can be altered. The pursuit of higher production need not be carried on at the neglect of environmental and social values. If it is, society will be failing to get optimal use from the two instruments at its disposal.

The foregoing analysis of the proper use of policy instruments in attaining the objectives of society rests on the assumption that the effects of employing a particular policy instrument are known. As a first approximation, this is a reasonable assumption. The unquestioned fact, however, that the effects can never be known with complete precision has interesting consequences that can be further analyzed. This takes us into the area of decision making under uncertainty.

Theorems in this area acquire particular importance when it can be assumed that the decision maker is averse to risk. When the decision maker is the community at large, the assumption of risk aversion seems plausible. For each individual, risk aversion follows logically from the familiar observation that rising income has diminishing returns, i.e., every additional dollar of income adds a little less than its predecessor to the total utility enjoyed by the recipient. A community composed of such individuals should also be risk averse.

Given this characteristic, society can reduce its risk of failing to achieve any one objective by employing the two available instruments simultaneously. In pursuit of a healthy environment and social justice, it will rely only in part upon government, placing some trust also in the voluntary action of corporations. This does *not* mean that the government employs corporations as its agents in addition to acting directly. It implies that society relies upon the social consciousness of corporations independently of what the government may do to guide corporate action in this regard.

This procedure will pay off provided that the success of government and corporations in achieving the objective is less than perfectly correlated. In other words, if adequate performance by government always means equally inadequate performance by corporations, and vice versa, then society really has but one instrument rather than two. It cannot reduce its risk by employing both simultaneously. What reason is there for assuming that society's trust in government and in corporations, respectively, will not always be disappointed or rewarded in exactly the same degree? If, for instance, government fails to do its proper job in this respect, does that increase or reduce the likelihood that corporations will also ignore the environment and social equity? Or should one expect that concern or neglect by one agent is likely to be associated with the reverse on the part of the other?

There is no general answer. The fact, however, that there is disagreement about whether corporations should have a role in the pursuit of social objectives suggests that there is uncertainty over what can be expected of government. There is no particular reason to expect negative correlation, i.e., that government will perform well whenever corporations perform badly, and vice versa. Some degree of independence can reasonably be assumed, however, with regard to government and corporate performance—either may perform well or badly regardless of how the other performs. Hence, the rule that diversification pays seems to apply also in the case where society must decide whether to pursue its objectives with one instrument or two.

Externalities

The presence of externalities, positive and negative, causes the allocation of resources by the market to deviate from the social optimum. If the production of electric power causes air pollution, failure of this negative externality to be included in the price paid by the user causes the private cost of power to fall short of the social cost. Too much power will be produced as a result. If the firm beautifies its plant, the social return on the investment will exceed the private return that the firm can appropriate. This positive externality causes private return to fall short of social return. Not enough beautification will be undertaken in consequence.

The remedies for positive and negative externalities are familiar: tax power, and subsidize beautification. Given today's increasing pressure on the environment, the frequency and magnitude of gaps between social and private cost or return are probably increasing. Actions which, in a richly endowed and not fully used environment, were innocuous, now produce damage. This creates problems for the market economy, and gives new scope to its critics.

Under these circumstances, public action to internalize externalities becomes increasingly urgent. This is one of the main planks in a constructive program to involve corporations. But to the extent that such a program rests on government initiative, we are not here concerned with it. In such programs, corporations simply respond. They do not exhibit social responsibility.

There are, nevertheless, ways in which corporations can take the initiative to achieve internalization. These are: (1) pressure on government to pass appropriate legislation, (2) cooperative action by groups of corporations and (3) recognition by corporations that the interest of stockholders with diversified portfolios goes beyond the profit maximization of any one corporation.

Pressure on Government

Suppose a firm found that a general anti-pollution campaign in its industry or neighborhood would so improve working conditions and labor supply that the investment would pay off, in financial terms, provided other firms participate. Alone, it cannot influence the environment sufficiently to make a difference from which it could adequately profit. One possible approach would be for this and like-minded firms to request the authorities to impose by law an investment that would benefit them all financially. This is one form of exerting social responsibility.

The firms would be better off if the depollution ordinance took the form of a tax instead of regulations determining maximum admissible pollution. Different firms may encounter different costs in cleaning up. An equal standard for all would be expensive to achieve for some, inexpensive for others. A tax on pollution would cause those firms which could afford it to stop polluting altogether. The rest could choose to pay the tax. If the tax is set at the proper level i.e., at a level that in the aggregate would motivate a sufficient degree of depollution, its objective will be achieved at minimum aggregate cost.

Responsible corporate action therefore can take the form of promoting not only action by government in general, but also action of the most economical kind. The use of anti-pollution taxes is not at present popular with environmentalists, who regard such a tax as a "license to pollute," which indeed it is. The price is the essence. Business also seems to be skeptical of a tax as opposed to regulation. But where there are significant differences in cleanup costs, the high cost polluters clearly will find it in their interest to be subjected to a flexible tax rather than to an inflexible ceiling.

Cooperative Action

In the situation described, the firms involved may also consider the possibility of forming an agreement. The content of this agreement might be that all firms would establish equal standards of depollution, or that all would incur equal or proportionate costs. The latter would be the more economical solution. Both solutions, however, raise questions under the antitrust laws.

Under these laws, trade associations and related activities among firms of an industry are of course permissible. They must not, however, facilitate anything in the way of a restraint of trade, including joint price setting. Action that would increase costs, such as a cooperative cleanup campaign, might be interpreted as having the effect of raising prices. In a competitive market, a single firm could not charge an increase in costs to the customer. All firms in the industry could, however. If success attends the effort to reduce pollution and thereby improves working conditions and the labor supply, costs and prices would not increase. But evidently some subtle questions of antitrust policy are involved. A court decision, like that in the case of *A. P. Smith* v. *Barlow,* which opened the door to large scale corporate giving to educational institutions, might clear the way here.

The Diversified Stockholder

Recognition that the stockholder with a diversified portfolio has a broader range of interests than the maximization of the profits of any one corporation, represents a third avenue toward the internalization of externalities.

Suppose a firm finds that investment in the training of unskilled labor would pay off, provided the workers acquiring new skills would stay with the firm permanently. If they leave and go to a competitor, the firm does not realize any return on its investment. But the competitor does, and if the stockholder owns stock in both firms, he will get his return from one firm or the other. The first firm would deprive the stockholder of a feasible return if it failed to make the investment in training, regardless of whether it or the competitor reaps the benefits.

Two assumptions underlie the analysis here summarized.[1] In the first place, the benefits from socially oriented expenditures must be "appropriable" by the corporate sector, i.e., they must show up somewhere on business income statements as an increase in profits. (Externalities that cannot be appropriated, such as better quality of life not expressed in higher productivity or improved labor supply, however desirable, pose a different problem.) The second assumption requires all stockholders to have shares in all corporations. In this limiting case, it can be shown that even the presence of corporations that refuse to engage in socially oriented expenditures and that thereby steal a march on their competitors does not alter the conclusion that each stockholder's financial interest requires each corporation to engage in socially oriented expenditures so long as there is an appropriate net return to the corporate sector as a whole.

For unappropriable externalities—"better quality of life" —the matter is more complex. Of course stockholders benefit, along with others, from the better quality of life, but as individuals, not as stockholders. Consequently, whether social expenditures by a corporation in which they own stock put them ahead or not depends on the amount of stock they have in each corporation. With respect to externalities of this kind, therefore, stockholders will disagree as to whether particular socially oriented expenditures should be undertaken or not.

Moreover, the treatment of hold-outs that refuse to engage in such expenditures becomes more difficult.

Dropping the second assumption—all stockholders owning some part of every company—further reduces the precision of the analysis. We then must consider the degree of risk aversion of individual stockholders, greater risk aversion requiring a more complete degree of diversification. Different stockholders accordingly will find themselves differently situated with respect to these broad externalities.

The analysis assumes that corporations act in the interest of their stockholders, which they recognize to be broader than the interest of any single corporation. Stockholder instructions to the corporation may be required to make corporations properly responsive to stockholder interest. The present widespread effort of some stockholders to alert corporations to their moral concerns is an instance of such stockholder behavior, although it is concerned typically with moral issues rather than with maximizing stockholders return on utility.

The Continuity of Corporations

In textbook economics, a firm produces a product over whose demand it has no control. When the demand disappears, the firm presumably closes up shop. This picture may not be altogether unrealistic with respect to railroads and other regulated industries, whose regulatory authorities do not permit diversification. But the ordinary unregulated firm, particularly when it is large and not a "one man" firm, seeks continuity. Stockholders come and go, but the corporation goes on forever.

Greater continuity implies two things. First, the interests of the corporation become more oriented toward the long run. Short run profit maximization may be harmful to long term survival. Recognition of social responsibilities may give the corporation the kind of acceptance in the community that it needs if it plans to be an ongoing operation.

A second implication is the expectation of the community that a corporation will have to act more along the lines of the community's interests if it wishes to have continued existence independent of its function as supplier of some product that the community may cease to want. While this expectation of the community is not compelling, I find it persuasive.

One way of expressing this is to say that the corporation's enlightened self-interest has changed. The "enlightened self-interest" concept has given rise to a great deal of fuzzy thinking, and, therefore, I do not want to employ it here. The enlightened self-interest of a corporation should require it to do certain things that pay off in dollars and cents. Of course this computation usually is very difficult to make. As a result, "enlightened self-interest" tends to become a catchall phrase for a lot of things that redound to the benefit of the corporation, but which have no basis whatever in a cost-benefit calculation. That is not the "enlightened self-interest" here referred to. Though the computation may be vague, it must make plausible that the rate of return is adequate. Whether the community's desire to have corporations engage in socially oriented activities is justified is of course a question as yet not fully resolved. It is the question we are debating today.

I would argue, however, that the mere fact that the community desires it makes a strong prima facie case. The contrary case would have to be very compelling to overcome this presumption.

"Stockholders' Money"

Discussions of social expenditures by corporations habitually run in terms of the appropriate use of "stockholders' money." It is taken for granted that the stockholder bears the cost, and that this could constitute a legitimate objection to this kind of corporate spending.

It was already pointed out above that this view is highly misleading, at least as far as the effects of the corporate income tax are concerned. At a 48 percent corporate rate, the federal government matches the corporation's funds almost dollar for dollar. The government in fact contributes massively while leaving to the corporation the decision over the use of funds. As a means of decentralizing the administration of social programs, and of strengthening a pluralistic society, this arrangement has much to commend it. And it just happens to make 48 percent nonsense out of the claim that corporate social expenditures are financed with stockholders' money.

How about the other 52 percent? If the corporation is the only one in its industry to engage in these expenditures, or engages in much larger expenditures than its competitors, it probably cannot shift the cost. It is then operating with stockholders' money. If, through cooperation, government requirement, well understood stockholders' interest, or in the corporations' own long term interest, all or most of the firms in an industry engage in similar expenditures, the cost curve rises, and the cost of doing good becomes a cost of doing business. Contrasting this situation with the alternative, in which the government performs the same socially oriented actions out of taxpayers' money, it is clear that the stockholder may find corporate responsibility a highly rewarding way of getting the nation's social work done.

The Role of Executives

Unlike the stockholder, the executive does not benefit from a diversification of interests. Nevertheless, the social involvement of his corporation holds out many attractions for him, too. He is now called upon to make judgments that go far beyond the task of allocating resources in the interest of profit maximization. Instead of being the employee of the stockholders or directors, he becomes an arbiter among competing interests—stockholders, customers, workers, society. This is a heady combination, and it would be surprising if executives did not find it attractive. In particular, young people who look askance upon business jobs, may find that this kind of orientation suits them.

The arrangement has the political advantage of shifting from the public to the private sector activities that should be performed with maximum economy rather than maximum bureaucracy. It fits into the design of a pluralistic society seeking a high degree of decentralization. On the other hand, it bestows considerable uncontrolled power upon corporate executives. The line of accountability becomes unclear. The question of the competence of corporate executives in handling social tasks must be raised. To judge by the great interest that executives have shown in the development of corporate social responsibility, it seems clear that they find the attractions outweighing the disadvantages.

Methods of Implementation

It is evident that large parts of the community today expect corporations to shoulder some social responsibilities. The classical reply that business best discharges its responsibilities by maximizing profits under conditions of competition is unconvincing to many people. In part, to be sure, this reflects erroneous conceptions about corporate profits that fail to take account of the role of profits as a measure of performance and as a source of necessary investment. But on the other hand, these are not the only aspects of profit. Somebody benefits in a more direct sense.

The argument cited in this paper concerning the role of the diversified stockholder demonstrates that even at the theoretical level profit maximization by the individual firm is an inadequate principle. The issue is not how wide a gap this analysis opens between maximization on behalf of the corporation and maximization on behalf of a diversified stockholder. The fact that there is such a gap—regardless of its size—is important. Nor need one assume that the market will quickly bring about a corporate reorientation in the interest of the diversified stockholder. The fact that in the long run such a tendency should exist justifies corporate efforts to bring about the results more quickly. It also justifies, of course, stockholder activism in persuading corporations of the need to face up to their responsibilities toward diversified stockholders at a minimum.

Consider the mundane consequences of corporate noncompliance. Business today is under critical scrutiny. A refusal to be responsive, however sincerely or adroitly supported by the classical defense of profit maximization, would be hard to sell. The result might well be legislation in the form of taxes and regulation, that in effect would be punitive. A strong anti-business movement in the country would indeed provide evidence that social involvement would serve the long-run interests of business. One might add that, in an age which demands more than goods and services, the insistence of corporations on being nothing but producers of goods and services threatens to force corporations increasingly out of the main stream of American life and into irrelevance.

The means for injecting relevance into the corporate scene, by the wrong route, already are on social reformers' drawing boards. This proposal for federal incorporation is one such device. Such a law would make corporations the creatures of the state with a vengeance. It would be a bad approach, because it would give the state enormous power without clearly specifying the purposes. As far as the achievement of particular objectives is concerned, it would mismatch instrument and objective. But this is the approach that corporate recalcitrance may provoke.

Many aspects of corporate impact on the environment and on society can indeed best be handled by legislation. Corporate management would be well-advised to give support to well-designed legislation. (To be sure, corporations cannot and should not be expected to support extremist legislation of this type.) Appropriate support would be one form of discharging its responsibility.

Cooperation among business firms as a means of reducing the competitive impact of socially oriented expenditures raises the question of relaxation of the antitrust laws. In the abstract, such a question is difficult to answer. Concrete applications and particular cases are needed to facilitate judgment. It should not be difficult for business to pose issues and develop possibilities in these terms, and give the public an opportunity to express its opinion.

For the stockholder, the social responsibility issue promises a real rejuvenation. Since Berle and Means, the stockholder has been regarded as basically functionless, a condition that does not bode well for the survival of private enterprise. In recent years, the cult of performance investing has made the relationship between the stockholder and his company even more tenuous. The new activism exhibited by some stockholder groups, on the other hand, promises a new lease on life.

This new activism, which has been in evidence at the stockholders meetings of many large corporations, is noteworthy as a form of social criticism that works within the system instead of trying to modify, if not to destroy, the system from the outside. It reflects the view, expressed above, that the interests of the stockholder are not necessarily those of the corporation, and that the corporation ought to heed these interests. In many cases, to be sure, the pressure of activist stockholders has not been solely or primarily toward socially oriented expenditures that could be appropriated by the corporate sector and that consequently would enhance aggregate profits. Very often, it has aimed at objectives that would enhance the well-being of the entire community, stockholders included, without showing up positively on earnings statements. But some rationale for this type of activism clearly exists in terms of the theory of the diversified stockholders' interest.

This activism contrasts sharply with Wall Street's traditional attitude toward stockholder criticism of management. "If you don't like the management, get out," has been the traditional reaction. This is purely defensive advice. Selling a stock is not a means of penalizing and thereby perhaps reforming the management. So long as a socially recalcitrant management makes money for its stockholders, there will be plenty of people willing to pick up the stock sold by social activists. There is little to be gained from an effort to create pariah corporations.

Nor is much to be gained from an attempt to influence corporations by mere token stock ownership. Groups of young people buying one share apiece in order to gain admission to stockholders' meetings are futile. Their well meant, but not always demonstrably rational, proposals merely strengthen the resolve of more substantial stockholders to send their proxies to the management instead of throwing them in the waste basket. As pointed out above, the interests of particular stockholders may differ on social activities not appropriable by the corporate sector. Small stockholders will tend to be more favorably inclined toward them than large stockholders because all get approximately the same benefits, along with the rest of the community, without all making the same financial sacrifice. But corporate law here seems to give exactly the right answer: The rule is not one man—one vote, but one share—one vote.

The movement to influence corporations by placing representatives of consumers, minorities and other watch dogs of all kinds on corporate boards, or by opposing and possibly overturning managements, clearly creates certain risks. Board meetings may become unproductive, management may be side-tracked in futile battles and corporate efficiency may suffer. But a careful and reasonable activation of the potential power of the stockholder need not lead to such consequences.[2] Large institutional investors, in particular, are unlikely to be swayed toward unreasonable action while, at the same time, they have all the more reason—because of their broader interests—to take action of some kind.

Whether based on the principle of diversified stock ownership, or simply a deepened sense of the responsibilities of ownership and trusteeship, stockholder activism has a strong economic rationale. At the same time, it augurs well for the adaptability of the corporate system to a more demanding world.

REBUTTALS

HENRY G. MANNE

Although Professor Wallich's paper contains several novel and imaginative arguments for corporate social responsibility, it fails, I think, to make the case for the doctrine.

Professor Wallich's analysis is seriously hampered throughout by a methodological weakness peculiar to many discussions of corporate policy. That is the practice of referring for all purposes to the corporate entity rather than to some individual human beings as the pertinent decision makers. Ultimately, only individuals have interests that can be rigorously analyzed with the tools of economics. While in the traditional economic theory of the firm, it is frequently legitimate to collectivize these individual interests into an abstract entity simply for methodological efficiency, this cannot logically be done when relevant conflicts exist between these corporate firm interests and individual interests.

For example, Professor Wallich refers to a case in his paper in which "the corporation may freely decide" to pursue some social purpose. But there is actually no such thing, apart from law and perhaps metaphysics, where this fiction serves a useful purpose. There is no such thing as a corporate decision, free or otherwise. This phrase can only be used harmlessly in a discussion of social responsibility when every individual shareholder would freely approve the transaction. Then, of course, we simply have a congruence of individual decisions that could be referred to as a corporate decision.

Professor Wallich gives us no idea of how many of the things that are sometimes claimed to represent corporate altruism he himself believes fit his definition of that concept. While he lists numerous areas of corporate responsibility—and that would seem to suggest that he believes there are significant amounts of it—his economic analysis actually implies very little. He gives us no clues to aid in resolving this apparent conflict. In connection with his use of target and instrument analysis, Professor Wallich seems to ignore the logical requirement that a specific quantitative goal be targeted. Unfortunately, he never shows how his goal can be identified, much less measured, nor does he suggest how we might quantify the comparative advantages of government and corporations.

Professor Wallich acknowledges that the effects of his model are uncertain and then oddly uses that conclusion to bolster his case for corporate altruism. To deal with the uncertainty (which he equates to risk) of obtaining social goals through government or private action, Mr. Wallich suggests that the risk can be minimized by diversification, presumably as with portfolio selection of risky securities. By combining government and business social activity in any proportion, we reduce the risk of failing to achieve an objective, such as production without too much pollution or clean air without too much loss of production.

Unfortunately, this risk diversification approach will not bear the intellectual weight put on it. The principal problem is that we cannot assume general agreement on social goals. And even if we do make such an heroic assumption, we cannot then assume that we will know the relative cost to be associated with the different risk approaches. Furthermore, various interdependencies and interactions between private and government actions really mean that we have no way of knowing if real diversification of risk can occur at all. We are not totally without information, but we lack the very kind necessary to use a risk diversification justification for the private production of public goods. In any event, the argument at most would tell us in which direction a vector points while giving no idea of the weight to be attached to it.

In connection with his discussion of externalities, Professor Wallich first identifies an actual socially responsible corporate activity: corporate lobbying to gain a governmental solution to a free rider problem in pollution control. This is spelled out in his main paper. His paradigm situation is one in which all the firms in an industry lobby the government to institute a user tax instead of a flat prohibition to control pollution. While Mr. Wallich argues that this solution would be socially optimal, he fails to note some interdependencies that would prevent this solution from occurring.

Some firms in the industry, those that would opt to pay no tax but would clean up all their pollution, may still prefer the flat prohibition precisely in order to prevent their competitors from opting for the right to continue polluting by paying the tax. Recognizing the latter as the preferred option of their competitors, these firms will lobby for a government system to make that impossible. There is no difference to them in the lobbying costs, and they can get a significantly better outcome. Professor Wallich offers no reason why we should anticipate this corporation's lobbying for its less desired governmental solution. Thus, even if he

67

has identified an area in which some general agreement within an industry or geographic area would be socially desirable, he tells us nothing about the feasibility of any particular agreement.

Professor Wallich's major economic argument for corporate social responsibility seems to be that relating to the appropriation of external benefits through concerted action on behalf of completely diversified shareholders. He acknowledges two assumptions underlying this argument, either one of which is so contrary to fact as to make the arguments either insignificant or completely wrong. The first of these is that the benefits from the socially oriented expenditure must be appropriable by the publicly owned corporate sector. Thus, if there is a substantial sector in which public stock ownership does not exist, as we know there is, there will be no way in which external benefits can be appropriated to even the most diversified of shareholders, since the nonpublicly held firms will continue to appropriate these benefits without incurring any costs. But to make matters worse, the main benefit to which Mr. Wallich refers—the value of higher skills imparted to workers—will in most cases be claimed almost completely by the worker as his wage increases to match his newer higher marginal productivity. Thus, the one big company scheme cannot really serve the purpose claimed at all. His second assumption, that all shareholders must have shares in all corporations, can only have significance if we posit a totally socialized "America, Incorporated," in which every citizen owns one nontransferable share. It is hard to see any significance to a corporate social responsibility concept based on this assumption.

By some unstated alchemy Professor Wallich seems to convert the current group of corporate activists into the diversified shareholders of his model—or maybe he merely hopes that they will be diversified. But he appears to miss the point of these current attacks when he characterizes them as the efforts of "some stockholders to alert corporations to their moral concerns." Moral concerns are still a long way from the opportunities lost because of incomplete investment diversification, and even casual observation of our corporate activists will show that their concern is in no sense related to their status as stockholders. They purchase their stock merely as a ticket that lets them freely and publicly voice concerns held prior to and independent of their status as shareholders.

Professor Wallich believes that stockholder activism has a strong economic rationale whether based on the principle of diversified stock ownership or on a deepened sense of the responsibilities of ownership and trusteeship. He tries, I think unsuccessfully, to show us how the economic rationale can be based on the diversification idea, but he does not even attempt to show how an economic rationale can be based on outsiders' deepened sense of responsibility.

In the last analysis, Professor Wallich tells us nothing about how a concept of corporate social responsibility can aid in the problem of defining, measuring and evaluating proffered solutions for social problems. He demeans the so-called "Wall Street Rule" of selling shares when one disapproves of management, while this scheme, in fact, offers the saving economic grace of a competitive market for what would otherwise be a system that could achieve neither economic nor social redemption.

HENRY C. WALLICH

As you have heard, Professor Manne takes exception to my theoretical argument on various points. I am grateful to him for pointing out one or two things in my paper that may require a more detailed statement. Broadly speaking, I don't think it affects what I've said and so I will not go into detail. Let me rather restate what I think is the main case against my argument, a case that for some reason, Professor Manne didn't make.

Typically, it is said that the corporation's business is to maximize profits because in doing so the invisible hand causes it to allocate resources optimally. And the making of maximum profits for the stockholders, hard as this may be to understand for non-stockholders, actually means that the production will proceed at the highest level of efficiency and resources will best be used. Now, this is respectable economic doctrine and it follows from it that the corporation should not concern itself with the quality of life, that it should not concern itself with the environment, with minorities or anything else. The government, if anybody, should concern itself with these things.

That argument, I think, is defective on several grounds. First, on its own ground, the assumption that the allocation of resources is optimal under a free market system is too narrow. Because of the familiar externalities—because such things as emissions of smoke, or the need to train people who could be useful in other firms, if not in your own, are ignored—the free market is far from a perfect allocater. Second, the income distribution that is brought about by this free market is very uneven. While I'd be the last to argue in favor of an even income distribution—I think unevenness has its function—nevertheless, one has to realize that the allocation of resources is in turn determined by the income distribution brought about by the market. If enough people make enough money so they can afford Rolls Royces, then the market will allocate resources to the production of Rolls Royces rather than to something that could be considered more urgent—and no slight is meant to that excellent automobile.

So, we start with a theory that is in itself debatable. The consequence of accepting that theory is, perversely, to achieve just the opposite of what most defenders of free markets and private enterprise want—namely, the consequence is to aggrandize the government. If the protection of the environment or the quality of life is left to government and if the quality of life becomes society's number one priority as against the mere production of routine goods and services, then government is rendered more powerful. The chance should be seized to cut down government, to reverse the trend and decentralize some of the functions of government to corporations as befits our pluralistic society.

I will grant Henry Manne that there are difficulties in making this case stick. But they are not nearly as great as he suggests. However, he has not really used any of these arguments, the traditional arguments, for his case. All he has really said is that we can't expect corporations to work for social purposes because if they tried they'd be taken over by a group of outsiders who would collect the necessary proxies by promising to make more money for the stockholders. Therefore management will never go in for a really thorough servicing of social responsibilities.

I suggest that this is a minute effect. You can trace it theoretically. As a matter of fact, takeovers don't come about for this reason. There are many corporations which engage in social expenditures and they are not in any danger of takeover. So, with recognition that this is an interesting line of argument, I would say it is not substantively very important. If a corporation is known to be doing what it should do to serve the people, to improve the environment, to improve the quality of life, it is utterly unlikely today that it will be taken over by a bunch of sharpshooters who tell the stockholders, "Give us control and we'll fire all the blacks, we'll stop the training, we'll pollute for all it's worth and we'll raise profits per share by $1.00." The trend is in the opposite direction. I doubt very much that any organized group of stockholders would have the courage to proceed in that ruthless way. If they tried, they'd be resisted by activist stockholders. And if the activists proceeded sensibly and realistically, if they did what the *Ethical Investor* prescribes, we should have no concern about either the inadequacy of corporate action or the danger of takeovers from insurgent groups. Thank you.

DISCUSSION

CLAUDE HOBBS, Westinghouse Electric Corporation: Professor Manne, as I understand your view, you believe business does what it must in producing social benefits in order to be thought socially acceptable. Professor Wallich evidently does not disagree, but he thinks that the benefit which flows from private business activity is as good as we can achieve from an economic system, and so let's not worry about the motivation. So I have two questions. One, do you disagree with my simplistic summary and if so, how would you change our economic and governmental system affecting business organization?

PROFESSOR MANNE: I have some difficulty with your summation of Mr. Wallich's point of view on this. I'm not quite sure how he deals with the question of the motivation of the decision makers involved. Indeed, all he purports to be doing as I understand it, is spelling out an economic argument for why private firms should voluntarily provide what we can term a public good, rather than simply directing all of their efforts to profit maximization.

The supposition here, although again it's not completely clear, is that we're confronted with some kind of market failure. We frequently hear the phrase "market failure." It's a shorthand way of saying "I don't like the distribution and allocation of resources and wealth that takes place in a free market system." It seems to me that in the market failures that we can honestly talk about—matters like pollution control—the government does have a special responsibility.

Under the scheme that Professor Wallich is posing for us, business would take on some of these traditional responsibilities of government. But it is not enough merely to say that it would be ideal to decentralize responsibility for these things by placing them in the hands of corporations. After all, these responsibilities can be decentralized by turning them over to other, responsible political units. Private corporations are not governments, they are not politically responsible, and I think that Professor Wallich would agree with me that we don't want to make them so.

Focusing on the last part of your question as it relates to corporate social responsibility: I think I can see very little room for change. The evidence of corporate responsibility that Professor Wallich and others seem to see all around us, I find simply as normal and rational business responses to government behavior or to the threat of government behavior. I see no evidence that corporations have really assumed this government responsibility.

Therefore, I can't propose anything very different for businessmen; I can't put myself in the position of saying that I know how to run your job at Westinghouse better than you do.

PROFESSOR WALLICH: Let me comment very briefly. If what I've said about socially oriented activities of business is not practicable, the role of the government will rise and will rise very rapidly. The range of functions that is open to corporations is shrinking relative to the total needs that people feel. Production of goods and services is no longer a top priority in this economy. So, if we say we cannot get corporations into the newer role of social responsibility, we're really saying we need bigger government. We are saying we need a society in which the free market has a reduced role and that of government bureaucracy and taxation grows apace. I prefer the other way, and I assume Professor Manne does too.

I have tried to provide what I think is a fairly solid theoretical basis for the idea that corporations, in the interest of stockholders, not their own, but in the interest of diversified stockholders, should do many of the things that are referred to as socially oriented. They would not be giving anything away, if they take into consideration the interests of the diversified stockholder.

Now what can we do in order to promote this action? It's essential that this kind of decentralized social action be promoted because the mechanism I've been describing, corporate action on behalf of the diversified stockholder, is one that, if implemented through the market, would take a very long time. Actually, mine is a normative proposition. It says this is the way things should work and will work in the long run. If corporations want to engage in these socially oriented activities immediately, here they have a theoretical justification. To be responsive to Mr. Hobbs's question about changes in our economic system, I would consider a very small one: there might be some relaxation of the antitrust laws that would allow corporations to cooperate in order to act jointly in social matters. This would preclude the recalcitrant, or maverick, corporation problem that might limit what other, more socially oriented corporations could do.

RICHARD FARRELL, general counsel, Standard Oil of Indiana: Professor Wallich, concepts, such as those in the *Ethical Investor,* now emanating from your eminent institution in New Haven, have intrigued me. And my question is this: Precisely how would you suggest that the ethical investor with a portfolio the size of Yale University's first define and then be satisfied as to the ethical standards of the management of all the companies in its investment mix? Or will it respond, on so-called ethical grounds, only when activist organizations are inclined to create an issue?

PROFESSOR WALLICH: Taking the second part of your question first, I think to respond only when activist organizations make an issue would be a weak-kneed policy. The ethical investor must take the initiative. On the other hand, I think the ethical investor will reject many of the proposals made by activists on the grounds that either they are very partisan proposals or that the damage that allegedly is being done is questionable. In any event, I think that the range of cases involving strong activist efforts—such as organizing a stockholders movement—would be small, and that such actions would be directed toward fairly obvious targets.

In general, I would hope that the ethical investor would take to heart the fact that when you've got a large portfolio such as Yale's, you are really so diversified that you can say you own stock in almost every corporation. In which case, everything that can be internalized by the business sector, even though not by any one particular corporation, becomes an internality to you—Yale—and justifies social action by any one corporation.

LEE LOEVINGER, attorney, Hogan and Hartson: Professor Manne, I'm somewhat concerned by what seems to me to be a rather artificial and too sharply differentiated categorization underlying your argument. If I understand correctly, you say that corporate social responsibility means voluntary or charitably motivated behavior which is differentiated from that which is coerced or economically motivated. Now, testing this proposition, I have recourse to your other principle, that ultimately only individuals have interests that can be rigorously analyzed by economic concepts. So, this leads me to this question: Under the laws of Maryland, where I live, and New York, where you live, the law requires that each of us provide the necessities of life to our respective wives and children. Now, let me ask you, do you provide your wife and children with the absolute minimum that the law requires or do you give them more than this? And if so, why? [Laughter.]

MR. GORALSKI: Is this a variation of the do-you-beat-your-wife theme—that is, do you beat your wife and children? [Laughter.]

PROFESSOR MANNE: No, he's simply asking an economic question: Does my wife have anything that causes me to give her more than the minimum that the law requires? [Laughter.] The answer is, you bet your life! [Laughter.]

Now a corporation will take certain actions if the government says it must or if, for instance, organized consumer pressures threaten. The corporation will take the action because it pays to do so and this activity can be fitted into a model of profit maximization.

Let me illustrate the point. Prior to 1954, and even more recently, we did not hear any of the vocal spokesmen or apologists for corporate social responsibility saying one word about racial hiring policies. One simply did not hear of it until it became a potential political issue, which eventuated in the Civil Rights Act of 1968 and, in many states, in FEPC laws. One did not hear anything about pollution control as a matter of corporate social responsibility until the 1960s when this concern for the environment began. We didn't begin to hear anything about it as a subject for voluntary corporate action until it was quite clear that government was going to step in. Thus it wasn't voluntary at all. So if we look at this whole issue from an historical perspective, we find no evidence for Professor Wallich's suggestion that these things are done out of a sense of altruism. Instead, what we find over and over again is that they are subtle and, I think, efficient market responses to inducements or pressures business faces.

VINCENT BURKE, *Los Angeles Times:* Professor Manne, you have told us to beware of altruism, that the motivation behind the behavior of corporate leaders is self-interest. My question is: Is there a significant difference in what motivates political leaders?

PROFESSOR MANNE: That is a nice question because I have one paragraph in my main paper that begins with a statement something like, "Political leaders like everyone else are interested in maximizing their own utility." I don't think there is much difference between the motivations of business and political leaders. Certainly, the model and the analysis that we would normally use for analyzing political behavior is somewhat different than that for analyzing market behavior. However, it is very interesting that in the scholarly literature these are beginning to coalesce, and we're seeing applications of traditional economic analysis to political phenomena. That's basically what I've done in connection with my longer analysis of the corporation; I tried to examine what the constraining influences are that operate on the real decision makers in the corporation. Professor Wallich suggests that he doesn't see these influences operating because he hasn't seen a tender offer or a proxy fight based on the fact that someone is engaged in alleged corporate responsibility. Of course, these takeovers do not deal with these issues. They are too small by themselves ever to count. What does count is the market value of the shareholders' stock. The available evidence is absolutely consistent with my proposition. In other words, the market for corporate control is working very effectively. We have a growing body of empirical data examining the functioning of the market for control of large corporations, and the evidence is coming in very strongly that the market is working as economic theory suggests it would. This in turn would explain why we haven't had the kind of fights that concern Professor Wallich. The social activity that is occurring is probably well understood by most business people to be profit-constrained behavior.

PROFESSOR WALLICH: We need to distinguish two kinds of approaches to the corporation. At one level we've got Professor Manne's, in which you have management separate from the board of directors and the board in turn separate from the stockholders, everybody pursuing his own interest. That is a corporate model in which the notion of maximizing profits no longer really exists. Management keeps the stockholders quiet and then pursues its interests with all its other constituencies: workers, customers, the government, and whoever else they may be. That is the model of the corporation which gives a great deal of leeway for socially oriented expenditures if the managers of the corporations so choose, because they are not under any maximizing constraints as long as they can keep the stockholders quiet.

The other model, which I used, is the traditional one of a corporation viewed as a unit in which management acts in the interest of the stockholders. If it deviates, it gets thrown out. In that case, it is assumed that the corporation either maximizes profits or it maximizes utility for the stockholders in some sense, but, at any event, always acts on behalf of the stockholders. My argument was based on this latter model, realizing that it has its limitations. But at any rate, it enables one to say something about this problem, whereas the "satisficing" corporate model leaves one with a completely indeterminate situation.

BARBER CONABLE, Member, U.S. House of Representatives: I'd like to say that these gentlemen are both very good advocates, and I think they may have overdrawn their case somewhat as advocates usually do.

It seems to me that we have another model, Professor Wallich, and that is the individual citizen. In an incentive system, there's not really that much difference between the corporate citizen and the individual citizen. We rely on the individual citizen to perform a substantial part of the pluralism of our society. It seems to me the answer in his

84

case is balance. He has to give his primary responsibility to his family, and of course, beyond that he likes to contribute something to his community. The corporate citizen should be in quite a similar position. But I think what constitutes balance is going to differ very greatly with the circumstances of the corporation, both economic and in regard to the community in which it is located. In this connection, I'd like to point out that Professor Manne's community of Rochester has two corporations that contribute very heavily to the community because their workers are very much concentrated in that community. And yet I would hesitate to say that it was entirely for purposes of self-interest that they contribute to the Rochester community. I think there it may be an enlightened self-interest, certainly, but that is the guide in achieving the kind of balance that we expect in a pluralistic society.

PROFESSOR WALLICH: It is indeed very difficult to distinguish between actions taken simply for public relations purposes, actions taken in the so-called enlightened self-interest—which means the longer run interest of the individual corporation—and actions taken along the lines that I am trying to describe, actions that are plainly not profit-maximizing for the corporation but which enhance the total profits of either the business sector or the welfare of the entire community. We have to realize that in every corporate action there may be various motives represented. That doesn't, I think, fundamentally change the analysis. What we need is a clear theory that says corporations should or should not engage in these activities, assuming we can describe them adequately. Now I take what Congressman Conable says to imply that he would say corporations should go quite far in finding a balance between corporate self-interest and good citizenship. This implies to me acting on behalf of either the whole universe of stockholders of all corporations or, going beyond, and acting on behalf of the community where it no longer benefits only stockholders but benefits everybody.

PROFESSOR MANNE: I think Representative Conable's point is a very interesting one. The concept of diversity is one that I think has come to occupy the attention not merely of the traditional conservatives in this country, but the more liberally inclined intellectual community as well. But I think it's also important to a careful analysis of the effects of decentralization of power, or the effects of any particular governmental conduct, to remember that there can be a very real difference between a corporation and an individual citizen.

We run into this problem primarily, and with what I think are incredibly damaging results, in the tax field. For tax purposes, corporations are treated as though they were individual citizens, without recognizing that a corporate income tax is visited in some way on one or another of the suppliers of goods and resources to corporations, whether it's the capital investors, laborers or other suppliers. We have the same kind of problem in the antitrust field. Careful analysis of many treble damage actions has revealed that their effects were visited on people who in no sense benefited by the original monopolization. Some of the same problems come up in the field of regulation of consumer goods, and so forth. So I think it's quite important, and I think it becomes of vast importance in dealing with the issue that Professor Wallich and I are addressing tonight, to recognize this distinction in connection with corporations. Ultimately, the real question in whatever we're proposing here is how it affects individuals and not how it affects some mystical or metaphysical entity that we call a corporation.

Representative Conable raised the interesting case of the quite evident and much renowned community behavior of the largest and second largest corporations in Rochester, New York and termed this enlightened self-interest. I would not disagree with that, while perhaps emphasizing it a little differently. Looking at major urban communities that have a large number of corporations, or at least no corporations employing as large a percentage of the total work force as does Kodak in the city of Rochester, we find that investment in community affairs is much less than Kodak's in Rochester. The reason isn't hard to determine at all. As Kodak invests in the city, they make it more attractive. This has the effect of lowering in some degree the direct compensation that must be paid to workers who come to Rochester with a high probability of working for Kodak. As you find this interest diffused by a number of large companies in a given community, you find less of such behavior. Now, Kodak's actions are certainly enlightened. I would call them good business. I also recognize that Kodak executives are quite sincerely altruistic, believing they are engaged in a kind of traditional community welfare program. But I also believe that the reason this community program survives is because it has been good business.

TED SUMBERG, Price Commission: Professor Wallich, you suggest that corporations should undertake socially oriented expenditures. Isn't this much easier in a monopolistic industry than in a competitive industry? In the second type, all the firms are very cost conscious. If one firm makes no such expenditures, and all the others make large expenditures, the first one will increase its market share and consequently, the others, observing this, will in self defense eliminate such expenditures. In other words, the norm for the industry will be established by the most flint-hearted corporation in that industry. In the case of a monopoly or oligopoly there are monopoly profits to distribute and if the three or four giant firms in the industry spend huge sums, so long as the differences aren't very great, they all can get away with murder. None of them will have any difficulty surviving and prospering. This is not the case under competition. Is this distinction correct, Professor Wallich?

PROFESSOR WALLICH: It has a correct component, in that a single firm in a competitive industry cannot deviate, in the direction of social responsibility, from the rest of the industry by as much as in other industries. But there is another side to the story, the case of a single firm rejecting the social orientation of all the rest of the firms. The problem with this recalcitrant firm, which I have called a maverick, is extensively dealt with in the paper. As long as you assume wide diversification of stockholdership, the maverick corporation is simply acting against the interest of its stockholders. If the stockholders are alive to what is going on, they will throw out the management, replacing it with management that will generate the externalities that are optimal for the diversified stockholder.

Now, if stockholders are not diversified, and if this maverick corporation is owned by, let us say, one stockholder who has no other holdings, then your case applies. In such an instance, we have to have recourse to a different theorem of economics, that of risk aversion: most stockholders are what economists call risk-averse stockholders, stockholders who will not put all their eggs in one basket. And, in a world of risk-averse stockholders, there is sufficient diversification to bring pressure on the maverick company to create the externalities that will be optimal for the diversified stockholder. I'm not saying that this will happen overnight, or even that you can observe the process over a few years. I believe this is a tendency that, in perfect markets, will make itself felt in the long run. This gives a corporation a justification for taking the action it wants to take—namely socially oriented expenditures—even in the short run. We need this kind of normative theoretical base. With such a base, let corporations proceed. I would expect to see socially oriented expenditures that are bona fide with very few ambiguities, self-seeking and falsification. I am not prepared to assume, as Professor Manne apparently does, that the dominant form of corporate social action is self-interested response dressed up as publicly interested response.

DICK JANSSEN, *Wall Street Journal:* Professor Manne, I believe you said that a corporation cannot feel a sense of social responsibility itself, but if its executives can, and act accordingly, in directing the corporation, what difference does that make?

PROFESSOR MANNE: In my paper, I tried to spell out what I thought were the economic parameters of something that we might really call corporate social responsibility. Interestingly, I came to very much the position that you're describing. Given some discretionary funds in corporations, and some feeling of benefit, or utility, or welfare, or freedom from pressure, on the part of executives, some of these funds will probably be used for what will be termed corporate social responsibility. This may indeed happen in another fashion as well, with the executives voluntarily deciding to make these expenditures out of what would otherwise be their own compensation. But we don't see too much evidence of that.

What I found is that corporate executives can be expected to behave as would any other person controlling approximately the same amount of discretionary funds. And when we look at the constraining parameters, we discover that the amount actually available for what we could meaningfully term corporate social responsibility, even in the largest corporation, is very, very small—so small as to be actually insignificant. That's not to say that some funds won't be used that way. It is to say, to go back to an earlier point, that it becomes extremely difficult to look at any particular transaction and guess (a) what the real motive of the decision maker was and (b) more importantly, what the economic ramification of the gift was. I think the economics of such situations strongly leads us to conclude that these are not charitable or altruistic activities on any really significant scale.

JAMES MILLER, American Enterprise Institute: I wonder if either Professor Wallich or Professor Manne would care to comment on the propensity of some large firms to heavily advertise their socially enlightened activities?

PROFESSOR MANNE: I can remember one case, many years ago. I'm sure many people in this room are familiar with the program that used to be called the Pepsi-Cola Scholarship Program. It was highly touted, at least in the high school that I attended in the 1940s, as one of the greatest things ever to come down the pike. It gave, in each state, two full-expense scholarships to any university a winner chose. Now, I have no doubt that the cost of publicizing that program exceeded by some several orders of magnitude the cost of actually giving those scholarships. That program has passed into corporate responsibility oblivion today, but it was once widely hailed as the epitome of corporate statesmanship. I suspect the same sort of thing is still going on.

PROFESSOR WALLICH: I think we have to distinguish between the analysis of corporate malfeasance, deceit, and bad publicity practices and the substance of my argument which assumes that executives, broadly speaking, are acting in the interests of their stockholders. Now, I am willing to grant to Professor Manne that there may be corporate deceit. There may be misleading advertising. There may be false motives in these activities. But let's look at that part of the activity which is not of that order and ask ourselves if it is justified. Unless Professor Manne can show that there is no reason why corporations should generate externalities that are in the interests of the diversified stockholder, I would say if they don't create them, they should. Their stockholders should make them do it. Evidence, if there is any, that they are not doing it is irrelevant to the normative determination of whether they should or not. Now, the question of how to divide the action into what is genuinely the socially oriented creation of externalities and what is merely self-seeking is

91

a difficult matter. I'm a little more charitably inclined than Professor Manne seems to be.

PROFESSOR MANNE: I want to make clear that I never said the motives were false or that any of this was deceitful. What I suggested is that people behave in accordance with their own self-interests. They may very well rationalize it. I think we all manage to rationalize what is in our own interest. That's a long way from suggesting that there's anything like conscious deceit involved here. But, good motives, like beggar's wishes, won't fly. The motive really has very little to do with it.

What really counts are the economic forces involved. And that's why I'm surprised to hear Professor Wallich continuing to press this issue of diversification of shareholder interests. Indeed, he now goes so far as to suggest that the directors have an obligation—presumably one that could be legally enforced—to engage in these activities that normally appear to be socially rather than profit oriented. His approach simply will not stand the pressure he's putting on it. At the very best, it covers a very small and perhaps insignificant range of current social interests. It does not cover the entire range of pollution problems, for instance. In the first place it is limited in geographical application. It would only cover, for example, the interest of the shareholders in corporations on one polluted body of water, say Lake Erie. But, the shareholders in those corporations would have no interest, even under Professor Wallich's theory, in having corporations avoid polluting rivers or streams elsewhere in the country.

There are other kinds of limitations as well. Expenditures to train workers, another social practice justified under Professor Wallich's theory, could actually be justified only if the training is not highly job specific. If it is, then the advantage claimed by Wallich could only be available to shareholders in corporations in the same industries. But in any event, this expenditure will never gain the benefit for shareholders claimed by Professor Wallich. Shareholders do not pick up the value of higher education for the workers. The workers alone pick up that benefit, unless it's highly specialized education that can't be transferred out of the particular firm that gives the training. Thus, in pollution controls and job training, the two areas in which the diversification point has most relevance, the practical effect is so small that I just don't understand Professor Wallich's argument that this justifies all corporations recognizing a duty to behave in this fashion.

DAVID MEISELMAN, Virginia Polytechnic Institute: I'd like to ask Professor Wallich a question that follows up on the comment of Professor Manne, having to do with Professor Wallich's presumption of proper behavior on the part of corporate executives, based on his analysis of the diversified interest of stockholders. Given the fact that stockholders do have diverse interests, I wonder how corporate executives can interpret exactly what those interests are. It seems to me that the difficulty of making such determinations is precisely one of the reasons that some of us like to think of individuals making a choice about the allocation of their income based on their own preferences and not turning this over either to a corporate big brother or a government big brother.

PROFESSOR WALLICH: This is a very real issue that Professor Meiselman raises, and I've tried to deal with it extensively in my paper. Briefly summarizing, my conclusions are these: So long as the externalities generated by a single firm accrue to the corporate sector, in other words are internalized by the corporate sector, there is a clear advantage to the diversified stockholder in having these activities carried out: he is, after all, interested in having bigger rather than smaller profits. The difficulty arises when you are thinking of externalities that accrue outside the business sector such as cleaner air, cleaner water, and so forth. Now, in these cases, stockholders benefit, and non-stockholders benefit, the benefits accruing to the stockholders in proportion to the amount of swimming and breathing they do, rather than in proportion to the amount of stock they own. Therefore, the problem Professor Meiselman poses can come into existence there— the interests of different stockholders are different. At that point, the result depends on the voting procedure in corporations which, as in government, presents the difficulty that the interests of the minority suffer in favor of the majority. But this is so pervasive a condition that I would not worry very much to find it happen in corporations.

CHARLES HOLT, The Urban Institute: I'd like to ask Professor Wallich several questions having to do with how the stockholder exercises his influence on corporations in the social responsibility area. One, if stockholders are highly diversified, they can't spend very much time really concerning themselves with what the corporations are doing. It's a real problem being well enough informed in order to know how to use their influence. Second, what kind of a role do you see the institutional investor playing? If the stockholder is removed from the corporation by an intervening mutual fund, how does he exert his influence? Perhaps there is a role of specialization here. And third, the Russian type of elections that characterize most American corporations, with a single slate of directors that are offered to the stockholders, gives a situation where there may be very little responsiveness to any stockholder vote.

PROFESSOR WALLICH: You point to communications costs or transactions costs which are real. The problem for the individual investor, I think, is not all that great. Most people, I presume, read their annual reports if they own their stocks directly. If they're in mutual funds, presumably they can either choose a fund that has declared its policy in these respects, or they can let the management know. This does not mean that they will prevail.

The greatest difficulty seems to me to arise in the very big range of stock ownership that occurs through pension funds. For example, if you work for General Motors and the General Motors pension fund is run by some bank or insurance company, how do you make your wishes effective? This is a problem of social engineering. I think we could all construct models in which a voting process could be instituted. We also know that it isn't going to work very perfectly. Maybe it's worth thinking about how progress could be made in that direction.

PROFESSOR MANNE: May I comment on the reference to Russian-type elections in American corporations. One hears this frequently. This idea finds its academic origins in the Berle and Means classic, *The Modern Corporation and Private Property.* I think it totally misses the point of the difference between a Russian election and a corporate election.

95

The great difference is that in Russia, if you don't like the results of the election, you are not free to leave. In a corporation, if you don't like the results of the election, you are very free to sever all connections with the company by selling your shares. Indeed, we have an incredibly liquid market in which you can sell those shares with great ease. We have a unique decision-making process in corporations which, strangely, is vastly more efficient as a democratic device than any political system which we could devise. It allows us to sell our votes for the price at which we're willing to have them shifted into the hands of another individual. We're not allowed to do that in the political sphere. The only comparable move that can be made in politics is to leave the jurisdiction. That in turn suggests one of the great virtues of our original federalist system in which there was some meaningful delegation of government power to states. The costs of severance become very much higher when there is one centralized government. And they become almost infinite when that government won't even allow some of its citizens to leave the country. The corporate system as we know it is almost the ultimate in decentralization and democracy. It works incredibly well to get the results that the real owners want because everyone is free to invest in the corporation that behaves exactly as he wants it to.

NORMAN TURE, economic consultant: Professor Wallich, I confess a good deal of confusion as to how your system is supposed to operate. On one hand, I think you have a great deal of trouble, as Professor Meiselman suggested, in suggesting how corporate management decision makers are supposed to identify the interests of the diversified shareholder, other than observing their behavior in the market place. From the point of view of the management of such a company, if that management is supposed to be responsive and undertake activities that are socially responsible, presumably the occasion for this is because there are externalities involved in its activities. My understanding is that an externality is really differentiated from an internality by virtue of the fact that the entity engaged in the activity generating the externality cannot measure those external benefits or costs. Indeed, the only reason they cannot measure them is because the marketplace does not cast up evidence to them about it. My question then is, what represents the guidelines for good behavior for the socially responsible corporation? You insist to Professor Manne that he has a "satisficing" model and you have a maximizing model. But it seems to me that unless, indeed, there are explicit quantitative constraints that are measurable by the decision makers, with explicit quantifiable benefits from the socially responsible action, you've got the satisfying model and he's got the maximizing model.

PROFESSOR WALLICH: You're looking at the micro-understructure, the accounting understructure of an economic process and, as we all know, our theoretical structures don't stand up 100 percent when we apply that kind of test. We talk of marginal cost pricing, but we know that firms don't know their marginal cost. We talk of marginal revenue and the demand curve, and we know that firms don't know their demand curves, and so forth. Nevertheless, the analysis seems sufficiently persuasive so that economists continue to use it. I don't even have to have recourse to Milton Friedman's positive economics concept that a model does not have to be realistic provided it predicts well. Given a principle such as I am proposing here, aiming at the normative, at something which ought to be done, if an action works in the right direction, there is a case for going ahead. In many cases, a fairly close computation of external benefits is quite possible. Moreover, many decisions are made and must be made without exact knowledge. For instance, we set standards to achieve certain environmental controls. Who tells us what level of pollution is tolerable, what level we ought to aim at? Who tells us what kind of a sulfur tax we should impose in order to achieve a certain level of cleanliness? All these are approximations. Trial and error will gradually get us into the neighborhood of equilibrium.

DR. TURE: Henry, I don't think trial and error will get us into the area of equilibrium. I think it will get us into the area of some disequilibrium to which there will be further response and adjustment. There is no a priori reason to believe, unless we have some way of measuring the externalities involved and the cost of being responsive thereto, for us to know whether or not any corporate action that is required or is initiated by the corporate management itself is in the direction of equilibrating or further disequilibrating. That is just a guess. Now that doesn't mean that government decision makers cannot exercise their preferences as to a state of affairs they'd like to see. But that has nothing whatever to do with maximizing with respect to anybody's utility function except those of the government decision makers.

Let me add something about your comments about marginal cost and marginal revenues and what models we must use. It seems to me that none of the theory presupposes that the business decision maker really has a precise measurement of his marginal cost schedule or of his marginal revenue and demand curve. All the theory really tells us is that we know what the conditions for profit maximizing are and the business entity is free to make mistakes and it will stop making mistakes and will maximize when certain conditions are met, i.e., the equality of marginal cost and marginal revenues. Precisely the same thing applies with respect to the externality argument.

PROFESSOR WALLICH: I would think that confirms my views. Externalities are treated like internalities. The firm cannot be precise but the process of trial and error gets it to the right point.

DR. TURE: The corporate decision maker doesn't know even the direction.

PROFESSOR MANNE: I'd like to give an illustration of Dr. Ture's point. I recently had occasion to ask an official of the Coca-Cola Corporation about their much publicized experience with improving the welfare of migrant workers in the orange groves in Florida. One of the things I was curious about was where these migrants came from. It turned out that they were originally dwellers in the malaria-ridden swamps of Georgia and North and South Carolina, apparently far away from any adequate educational facilities, housing facilities, medical care, or what have you, and that they became migrant workers because that, at least, was better than what they had in the swamps. Now, we're told that Coca-Cola expended some several millions of dollars, so I asked this official how Coca-Cola responded to this significant new cost. "Well," he said, "we've accelerated the introduction of automatic orange picking equipment." [Laughter.] I said, "Well, you must not employ as many migrants as you did?" "No," he said. They had substantially reduced the number of workers. And, then I asked him the question that he had never considered before: What happened to the ones that Coke no longer employed? He seemed visibly surprised as he replied, "Well, I guess they've gone back to the swamps."

Now, it's not at all clear to me that this episode of voluntary corporate altruism actually had the purpose that is alleged for it or that it even served the announced goal. It may very well have served to reduce rather than increase total human welfare.

JOSEPH ASCHHEIM, George Washington University: Professor Wallich, you speak in your paper of "society relying upon the social consciousness of corporations independently of what the government may do to guide corporate action." My question is: Who is society apart from the elected representatives of the body politic? And what is the distinctive expression of society as the elected representatives of the body politic other than the legislated rules and regulations of that society?

PROFESSOR WALLICH: By society I did not mean a body apart from the individuals constituting it. I meant the community, the citizens who express their views either through the political process or through the market process. When they instruct the corporations in which they own shares, their action is a political process in the private sector. I think of citizens as wielding two instruments: one is corporations, the other is government. Broadly speaking, they have the choice of employing either or both of these tools to pursue, in this case, two objectives, these being "production" and "quality of life." Then the question becomes the assignment problem familiar from the study of policy making: Should we assign to corporations only the job of production, to government only the job of raising the quality of life? Or do you aim both instruments toward both objectives? This is a part of economic theory that is well explored. We know also that the answers depend on the relationship of the tools—corporations and government—to the objectives— production and quality of life. This is simply an effort to apply a well-known principle of economic theory to this particular situation. You may say I've done the concept of "tools" a little violence, but it seems to me a reasonable liberty to take.

PROFESSOR ASCHHEIM: Well, I still have difficulty in identifying society in this context. As I understand it, your distinction between instruments and targets is simply the proposition that there is a division of labor between society or corporations on the one hand, and government on the other. You, however, seem to introduce some third element here which is, if not illegal, extralegal. And how is one to establish, to identify, this element? Where does one derive this from? When you speak of society, does one turn to the John Birch Society or to the Mont Pelerin Society? Where other than the rules and regulations that have been legislated by the elected representatives of the body politic on the one hand and, as you point out, by consumers or producers on the other hand, does one find the normative propositions that you favor?

PROFESSOR WALLICH: By society I mean the people, the people of the United States. They, by whatever means, through Congress assembled or as stockholders, lay down the rules and make decisions.

NOTES

NOTES TO FIRST LECTURE

[1] It should be noted that even if *all* firms in the industry voluntarily incur this same added unit cost, the effect will be the same as a tax on the industry, with long-run higher prices and lower production. In either case the wealth loss from all future anticipated contributions will be visited on the stockholders at the time the new activity and its consequences become predictable.

[2] As present managers perform less efficiently, the price of the stock declines but never to the full extent indicated by the inefficiency since the possibility of a takeover by more efficient management increases as the share price drops and thus provides some support for a higher price. But it is the possibility of substantial capital gains on shares that fuels most management-displacing takeovers. For a more detailed elaboration of this thesis, with applications for the various takeover devices, see Henry G. Manne, "Some Theoretical Aspects of Share Voting," *Columbia Law Review* (1964), vol. 64, p. 241.

[3] Actually *all* personal contributions as a percentage of gross taxable income are in the range of 3 percent, but the largest part of that was represented by gifts to churches, a type of donee rarely receiving corporate funds.

[4] "Social Responsibilities of Business Corporations," A Statement on National Policy by the Research and Policy Committee of the Committee for Economic Development, June 1971.

[5] Ibid., p. 59.

[6] Ibid.

[7] *Wall Street Journal,* April 24, 1972, p. 1.

NOTES TO SECOND LECTURE

[1] A fuller examination is provided in Henry C. Wallich and John J. McGowan, "Stockholder Interest and the Corporation's Role in Social Policy," *A New Rationale for Social Policy* (New York: Committee for Economic Development, 1970).

[2] Cf. John G. Simon, Charles W. Powers, Jon P. Gunnemann, *The Ethical Investor* (New Haven: Yale University Press, 1972).